let's talk!

Good stuff for girlfriends about
God, guys, and growing up

Danae Dobson

TYNDALE HOUSE PUBLISHERS, INC., Wheaton, Illinois

Library of Congress

Dobson, Danae.
   Let's talk! : the girlfriends' guide to God, guys, and growing up / by Danae Dobson.
      p. cm.
   Summary: Offers "big sister" advice, Christ-centered encouragement, and information for living confidently in today's world.
   ISBN 0-8423-0818-0 (sc)
   1. Teenage girls—Religious life. 2. Christian life. [1. Christian life.] I. Title.
BV4551.3 D63 2003
248.8'33—dc21   2002013750

Printed in the United States of America

09 08 07 06 05 04 03
7   6   5

DEDICATION

In Titus 2:4-5, we are told that the older women should teach the younger women. I am blessed to have a mature Christian mentor who has played this role in my life. Her name is Kathleen, and she has been a *wonderful* friend to me. She prays for me every day and has opened the Scriptures to me in a way that I didn't understand before. I love this special lady and thank God for bringing her into my life.

CONTENTS

INTRODUCTION

Do you ever wish you had someone you could talk to—about guys and girls, jealous friends, family feuds, how to make sense of your life, and how to really know God? I always wanted a friend or big sister who could clue me in on all the important things, including the best way to get a guy's attention! I needed someone who could relate to what I was going through as a teen. I grew up in a wonderful family, but I still struggled to find my place socially, just like every other teenager. It's something we all have to deal with. But sometimes a word or two of advice from someone who has "been there" can be helpful.

That's why I would like to be a kind of long-distance friend or "big sister" to you. Even if you already have a true friend or two, it doesn't hurt to have another one. In this book, I'll pass along some helpful tips that I've learned about God, guys, and growing up. There's so much for us to discuss that will relate to your day-by-day experiences. So, come on, girlfriend . . . let's talk!

Danae Dobson

Danae Dobson

Check It Out!
PHILIPPIANS 2:1-5

One of the mottoes that I live by is this: Be in the world, but not of the world. That doesn't mean I never listen to secular music or go to movies, concerts, and sporting events. I think it's acceptable to engage in some of the world's pleasures, as long as they're not sinful (chocolate excepted). Only now I'm more conscious about how I spend my time. I find myself frequently asking the WWJD question: "What would Jesus do?"

You may have seen the letters WWJD on rings, bracelets, and necklaces. They're not as trendy as they were a couple years ago, but the concept they convey is important. WWJD is a good question to ask as we make our daily decisions.

Recently, a girlfriend told me that her husband had been invited to a Korn rock concert. He had decided to go, and my girlfriend was unhappy about it. She didn't feel that this type of atmosphere was appropriate for a Christian. I had to agree. The reason is that Korn's music has anti-God/anti-Christian lyrics. Jesus wouldn't go to this type of concert, so why should we?

Some people argue that the reason for going into a worldly environment is to "witness" for Christ. What kind of witness is it to be seen where God's name is being dishonored and immorality promoted? Can you imagine Jesus going to a place like an anti-Christian rock concert except to condemn it? I don't think so! The apostle Paul told us to "abstain from all appearance of evil" (1 Thessalonians 5:22, KJV).

Before deciding to go somewhere controversial, think it over! Ask yourself these questions:

- What is my purpose in going?
- Would Jesus feel comfortable in this environment?
- Have I prayed about this decision?
- How can I have an impact on people for Christ?
- Will I face peer pressure and temptations that could make me feel uncomfortable?
- Will the environment harm me spiritually?

I understand how difficult it can be to turn down an invitation when you *really* want to go. Thoughts run through your mind like "All my friends will be there!" and "I'll feel left out if I stay home."

Why is it unwise to hang out with unbelievers and people who compromise? As long as you're avoiding sin, does it really matter if you get as close to the world as possible? The Bible speaks directly about this subject in 1 Corinthians 15:33, which says, "Do not be misled: 'Bad company corrupts good character.'" Just like gravity, you have a greater chance of being pulled down than of being lifted up. By "hanging out" with unbelievers and people who are not strong Christians, we expose ourselves to temptations that might weaken our resistance. Human beings are, after all, social creatures. We are inclined to follow the herd. As the prophet Isaiah put it, "We all, like sheep, have gone astray, each of us has turned to his own way" (53:6). That's why it's important to prayerfully consider the WWJD question (along with the others listed above).

Asking "What would Jesus do?" is not only helpful in the context of choosing friends and activities but also in many other situations. Here are some examples:

- If someone hurts your feelings, WWJD?
- When you're tempted to compromise your beliefs, WWJD?
- If you're angry and want to take it out on someone, WWJD?
- When you see a person in need, WWJD?

We find the answers to these questions in the New Testament. It is here that we understand who Jesus is and how we can model our life after Him. As Paul wrote in Philippians 2:1-2, "If you have any encouragement from being united with Christ, if any comfort from his love, if any fellowship with the Spirit, if any tenderness and compassion, then make my joy complete by being like-minded, having the same love, being one in spirit and purpose."

Our goal should be to imitate Christ! That's why the WWJD question is important—it holds us accountable. Of course, we're going to stumble now and then, but we should *strive* to be perfect, as He is perfect (Matthew 5:48).

Have you considered what a privilege it is to have a personal relationship with Jesus? To know He has forgiven all your sins and to be able to communicate with Him at any time? When we really know Him—really love Him—we want to be found blameless in His sight. There's no greater joy or satisfaction! Everything hangs on that one question: WWJD?

your turn

❶
Describe a time when you made a moral decision based on your relationship with the Lord (for example, whether or not to attend a drinking party).

❷
What can happen to a Christian who socializes with unbelievers?

❸
What are some ways you can imitate Christ in your life?

CUT!

Check It Out!
PSALM 101:3

It began as just another night at the movies. Some college girl-friends and I drove to the local theater to check out a popular comedy. When we got there, I recognized three guys from school. They happened to be sitting in the row behind us, so we chatted with them awhile before the show started.

Thirty minutes into the film, I was feeling pretty uncomfortable. We had already heard foul language and sexual jokes and witnessed a couple of tasteless scenes. It was about this time that I turned around to say something to one of the guys. I was surprised to see that all three of them were gone! They had walked out of the theater, obviously as a result of the disturbing content.

Their response had a profound impact on me. I really admired the guys (football players, no less!) for adhering to their convictions. It also provoked some interesting thoughts: 1) Was there a standard that all Christians should follow? 2) Shouldn't my girl-friends and I have walked out, too? 3) Why were we still watching the film? Since that experience, I've become much more selective when it comes to movies.

Now don't get me wrong—I *love* a good movie! The right one can make you laugh, cry, or even transport you to another place in time. It can inform, instruct, change your way of thinking (for the better), and leave a lasting impression. Over the years, there have been a number of films that have affected me this way.

On the other hand, let's admit that there's also some pretty terrible stuff out there. Here's where discretion comes in. We need to make a conscious decision about what types of films are off our must-see list.

Whenever I go to the video-rental store, I'm amazed by some of the junk that's on display. Words like *nudity, strong language,* and *violence* are frequently used to describe subject matter. The other day I pulled a popular video off the shelf and read the back. This was the basic premise: A teenage boy and girl make a bet about whether or not the boy can get the school principal's virgin daughter to sleep with him. If he succeeds, he also wins the right to have sex with the girl he made the bet with. How's that for a raunchy plot?

Another disturbing aspect of today's movies is how often Christianity is made fun of. Jesus is our Savior and Friend—it's up-setting to see Him mocked or to hear His name raked through the gutter. This sort of thing seems to be occurring more frequently these days. A number of films I saw this year included one jab or another against Christ.

So what do you think is required of us in regard to entertain-ment? One thing is certain—Psalm 101:3 makes it very clear when it says, "I will set before my eyes no vile thing." That means we must decide ahead of time not to watch anything evil or obscene. We can't always know the content before we see a movie, but in most cases we have a pretty good idea.

Not long ago I became interested in foreign films. I began renting various titles, selecting those that had been applauded by the critics. Not surprisingly, I found some of the videos pretty trashy. The Lord brought one word to my mind: *discretion.* I was not exercising good judgment when renting these foreign films; I needed to be more discerning.

You might be asking, "What's the big deal, anyway? It's only entertainment—why does it matter what we expose ourselves to?" Let me try to explain with a story.

A father of three teenagers set a rule that the family could not watch R-rated movies. This created a problem when a certain popular movie opened in local theaters. All the teens were bent on seeing the film, despite its "R" rating.

The teens interviewed friends and even members of their church to compile a list of pros and cons about the movie. They hoped that the list would convince their dad that they should be allowed to attend.

The cons were that it contained only a few swear words that misused God's name, only one act of violence ("which you can see on TV all the time," they said), and only one sex scene (and it was mostly implied sex, off camera).

The pros were that it was a popular movie—a blockbuster. If the teens saw the movie, then they would not feel left out when their friends discussed it. The movie contained a good plot and two hours of nonstop action and suspense. There were fantastic special effects! The movie also featured some of the most talented actors in Hollywood. The teens were certain that the film would be nominated for several awards. And Christian friends at their church who had seen the movie said it wasn't "that bad." Therefore, since there were more pros than cons, the teens asked their father to reconsider his position just this once.

The father looked at the list and asked if he could have a day to think about it before making his decision. The teens were thrilled. *Now we've got him!* they thought. *Our argument is too good! Dad can't turn us down!* So they agreed to give him a day to think about their request.

The next day the father called his three teenagers, who were smiling smugly, into the living room. They were puzzled to see a plate of brownies on the coffee table. The father said he had decided that if they would eat a brownie, then he would let them go to the movie. But just like the movie, the brownies had pros and cons.

The pros were that they had been made with fresh walnuts and the finest chocolate. These moist frosted brownies had been created with an award-winning recipe. Best of all, they had been made with care by the hands of the teens' own father.

The brownies had only one con. They had a little bit of dog poop in them. But the dough had been mixed well—the teens probably would not even be able to taste it. And their father had baked the brownies at 350 degrees, so any bacteria or germs had probably been destroyed. Therefore, if any of his children could stand to eat a brownie that included "just a little bit of poop," then they also would be permitted to see the movie with "just a little bit of smut." By now the teens had lost their smug expressions. They turned down the tainted brownies, and only Dad was smiling smugly as they left the room.

Now when his teenagers ask permission to do something he is opposed to, the father just asks, "Would you like me to whip up a batch of my special brownies?"

Philippians 4:8 says, "Whatever is true, whatever is noble, whatever is right, whatever is pure, whatever is lovely, whatever is admirable—if anything is excellent or praiseworthy—think about such things."

It's hard to concentrate on things that are noble and lovely while watching a smutty film. In fact, let me ask you this question: Have you ever felt kind of "dirty" when you walked out of a theater? You know, the feeling that comes after hearing one cussword after another and seeing ten characters murdered in cold blood? If you've felt that way, it was because your mind was filled with impurities—you were being consumed by wicked images.

This same principle applies to reading material, music, the Internet, and television shows, too. Recently, *Entertainment Tonight* pointed out that TV sitcoms are now "pushing the envelope" with indecent programming to compete with cable stations. Funny, I can't think of a time when they didn't cross boundary lines, can you? Most sitcoms do not cause us to think about what is true, right, and pure.

The bottom line is that those who love the Lord and want to please Him should "keep [themselves] from being polluted by the world" (James 1:27). If we're exposing our minds to violence, sex outside marriage, greed, foul language, and other worldly sins, is there any room left to be filled with the Holy Spirit? Can we truly experience satisfaction in our communion with God? Think about it.

your turn

①
Why is it important to use discretion when it comes to music, books, TV programs, the Internet, and movies?

②
If your friends asked you to see a raunchy movie with them, what would you say, and why?

③
How high are your standards regarding entertainment? What do you think God's standard is for you?

PARDON MY "FRENCH"

Check It Out!
PSALM 19:14

What do you say when you stub your toe or slam a door on your finger? In moments like these, you gotta say *something!* It just isn't natural to remain silent. I'm sure there are some folks who express their discomfort with a simple "Ouch!" but I'm not one of them. You probably aren't either. "Ouch!" is too mild when you're doubled over in pain.

Maybe that's why some people shout obscenities. Something about screaming the nastiest word that comes to mind just seems to get the point across. Swearing is inappropriate for a Christian, of course, so some of us spout off a string of ridiculous words that don't make any sense.

The other night, I ran barefoot into the cat's scratching post. Are you aware that those carpeted pillars have a hard piece of wood underneath? My poor toes! I think I muttered every *non-cussword* I could think of as I collapsed in agony. For the rest of the night I had to hobble on one foot because it hurt to walk. If there was ever a time to rattle off a string of obscenities, that was it! The next day my toes were a vibrant shade of purple—a tribute to my clumsiness.

One doesn't have to be in anguish to feel tempted to cuss, though. I hear bad language in all kinds of settings—everything from relaying humor to telling a story. Just today I overheard two guys talking while I was getting my car serviced. One of them chuckled and said a four-letter word in connection with his soft-drink cup. I could tell that he thought nothing about what he said—it was just everyday conversation to him.

Why do you think profanity is so common? I think it's fair to say that some of the responsibility goes to the film industry. I have seen movies where bad language was used in almost every scene.

The interesting thing about foul language in movies is that it serves no purpose. Yes, I've heard the argument about the importance of realistic characters, but that doesn't justify swearing. I've seen many powerful, award-winning films that didn't have cusswords. Besides, people do all sorts of disgusting things in real life, but we don't want to spend our money to watch them do it. So why would we want to watch realistic characters cuss and swear for two hours?

Peer pressure is another contributor to the widespread use of profanity. When your friends are saying four-letter words on a regular basis, it seems natural to incorporate them into your own vocabulary. It's the old "everybody's doing it" rationale. For whatever reason, the use of profanity seems to be increasing in our culture. I'm sure you hear it almost every day at school, in your neighborhood, or on television. When a person is exposed to "gutter language" over a period of time, a process known as *desensitization* occurs. This means that the shock effect is gone—what was once appalling now seems normal. We have become a nation of foul-mouthed people!

Did you know that God is very displeased by the crude way we talk? That is what we read in His Word. Consider these passages:

- "Do not let any unwholesome talk come out of your mouths, but only what is helpful for building others up according to their needs, that it may benefit those who listen" (Ephesians 4:29).
- "Nor should there be obscenity, foolish talk or coarse

joking, which are out of place, but rather thanksgiving"
(Ephesians 5:4).

- "May the words of my mouth and the meditation of my
  heart be pleasing in your sight, O LORD" (Psalm 19:14).

As you can see, the Bible is very clear about God's expectations. He wants us to be conscious of what we say and to bring
glory and honor to Him with our words.

This raises a very important point: Some Christians feel comfortable using the phrase "Oh my G——!" in casual conversation. I
cringe when I hear people use the Lord's name disrespectfully, and
I wonder if they know how He feels about that. Exodus 20:7 says,
"You shall not misuse the name of the LORD your God, for the LORD
will not hold anyone guiltless who misuses his name." This warn-
ing was significant enough to be included in the Ten Command
ments, so it must be taken very seriously by anyone who is trying
to do what is right.

I once confronted a friend at school about this. We were walking together after class, and she responded to something I said
with, "Oh my G——!"

"You shouldn't say that," I told her. "You're using the Lord's
name in vain."

"No, I'm not," she argued. "To use His name in vain means to
say it in *anger!*"

Perhaps some people would agree with this girl, but the Bible
doesn't say that. Here is another Scripture that refers to the reverence of God: "If anyone considers himself religious and yet does
not keep a tight rein on his tongue, he deceives himself and his religion is worthless" (James 1:26).

The Bible also says, "Let us purify ourselves from everything
that contaminates body and spirit, perfecting holiness out of reverence for God" (2 Corinthians 7:1). The way we talk reveals how
much (or how little) we respect our heavenly Father.

To sum it up, if you aren't talking *to* God or talking *about* Him,
you shouldn't be using His name. The same goes for Jesus Christ,
the "name that is above every name" (Philippians 2:9). He is the

Creator of the universe; the almighty King of kings and Lord of lords. Can we really justify throwing His name around as though it meant nothing?

Here's a question to ask yourself: Are the words of your mouth and the meditation of your heart pleasing to the Lord (Psalm 19:14)? If bad words have slipped out of your mouth lately, here's some good news: You can ask God's forgiveness and start again with a clean slate! God will help you avoid unwholesome talk and the temptation to swear—even when you drop a five-pound book on your toe!

your turn

❶
Do your friends use bad language? If the answer is yes, has their speech had an impact on you? In what way?

❷
How do you feel when you're in a movie theater and the name of Jesus Christ is used in a disrespectful way? Does it make you uncomfortable, or have you become desensitized?

❸
How can your choice of words be a witness to others?

WITHOUT CEASING

Check It Out!
1 THESSALONIANS 5:17-18

Do you believe prayer works? I mean, honestly, are you certain that God hears you when you talk to Him and that He answers you? Do you trust Him with your deepest longings and your secret fears?

Is He interested in our daily life and the challenges that we face? More importantly, does the all-powerful God of the universe actually desire fellowship and communion with us mere mortals? I remember my pastor saying that one of the hardest concepts to grasp is that we're actually being listened to when we pray. I can relate, because I used to wonder about that very thing as a teenager. I struggled with the fact that I couldn't see or converse with God. In my heart, I knew He was listening to every word I said, but a little shadow of doubt was in the corner of my mind. Do you sometimes feel the same way?

Well, let's see what the Bible says about prayer:

- "We do not know what we ought to pray for, but the Spirit himself intercedes for us with groans that words cannot express" (Romans 8:26).
- "Pray continually; give thanks in all circumstances, for this is God's will for you in Christ Jesus" (1 Thessalonians 5:17-18).

Prayer is not only honored by the Lord, but we also are commanded to enter into this personal communion with Him. And what a privilege it is for Christians! We don't need to make an appointment to get His attention. There are no receptionists or secretaries standing in the way. He never puts us off for a later time because He's too busy. Never! We have an open invitation to speak to Him whenever we please. Our God is always ready to listen. He can hear the faintest cry of the sick, the lonely, and the despised of the world—anyone who calls on His name. Each one of us who trusts in the Savior is known and loved by Him, in spite of our imperfection. Truly, the invitation to prayer is an expression of God's love and compassion for humanity. A precious gift!

For years a tiny needlepoint pillow has hung in my parents' living room. The phrase "Without Ceasing" is stitched on the front, taken from 1 Thessalonians 5:17 (KJV), which says, "Pray without ceasing." The little pillow symbolizes the importance of prayer in my family. It also represents my mother's influential role as chairperson of the National Day of Prayer. This significant event is held every year in Washington, D.C., and around the country on the first Thursday in May. It is my mom's responsibility to "rally the troops," so to speak, to pray for our leaders and our nation. She and her staff work twelve months a year to prepare for this one important day. Why all the effort? Because my mother and millions of other believers are convinced that prayer changes things. One of the verses that she frequently quotes is 2 Chronicles 7:14: "If my people, who are called by my name, will humble themselves and pray and seek my face and turn from their wicked ways, then will I hear from heaven and will forgive their sin and will heal their land."

Our land desperately needs healing! Crime and violence are on the rise, and families are hurting because of divorce, abortion, substance abuse, homelessness, sexually transmitted diseases, and homosexuality. None of these problems can be resolved any other way than through an appeal to our heavenly Father, who hears the prayers of His children. That's why the National Day of Prayer is such a worthwhile effort. Last year there were twenty thousand prayer events across the country, with two million people participating and forty thousand volunteers. A great volume of prayer ascended to the heavens on behalf of our nation. The Lord surely heard the voice of His people!

So let me ask you: What does prayer mean to you? Has there ever been a time when you cried out to Jesus and received His peace? Have you experienced an obvious answer to a prayer request? Do you know the joy of experiencing spiritual intimacy with the Lord?

In my own life, prayer has helped me to develop a relationship with God. I cherish the time that I spend with Him, talking about whatever is on my mind and listening for His voice. Sometimes I like to drive to my own special place in a quiet neighborhood. I turn off the engine and talk to the Lord. In between sentences, I pay attention to the "still small voice." This is my way of giving God an open invitation to speak to me if He desires. Over the years, He has brought many inspirational thoughts to my mind. I'm so glad I took the time to listen!

One thing that I've learned through the years is that prayer is not about getting what you want—it's about accepting God's will. I've been denied some requests that meant a great deal to me—things that I really petitioned for. Other times, I've been in the "waiting room" a lot longer than I would have liked. This is where trust comes in—banking on the promise that "God causes all things to work together for good to those who love God, to those who are called according to His purpose" (Romans 8:28, NASB).

I'll always remember something that happened ten years ago, while I was still in the "training stage." I was driving my car, grumbling and complaining to the Lord for not answering a year-long request. "Maybe I should just quit praying," I griped, almost like I was trying to punish God for His silence. "I've been praying and praying and nothing has changed. I feel like giving up!" Believe it or not, ten minutes later I passed a billboard with these words: "Don't give up! Pray! It works!" If you think that didn't send a chill down my spine . . . ! It seemed like a personal message direct from God to me, and I suppose that in a way it was.

Jesus actually taught a lesson about this very subject. It's the parable of the persistent widow found in Luke 18:1-5. In this story Jesus described a judge who didn't fear God or care about people. A widow in the town kept coming to him with this plea: "Grant me justice against my adversary." For some time the judge refused. Finally, he said to himself, "Even though I don't fear God or care about men, yet because this widow keeps bothering me, I will see that she gets justice, so she won't eventually wear me out with her coming!" (v. 5).

Jesus used this parable to teach us always to pray and not give up. If a corrupt judge would reward a woman for her persistence, how much more will God bring justice for His chosen ones?

Is there something you've been praying about that seems to have fallen on deaf ears? Don't give up! Rest on the assurance that Jesus loves you and His answers are worth waiting for!

your turn

❶
Do you talk to God on a regular basis? If not, why not start a routine by praying at the same time each day?

❷
Has the Lord responded to one of your prayers in a miraculous way? Describe what happened.

A CAT TALE

Check It Out!
MATTHEW 18:10-14

Have I told you about Kid-Wid? I haven't? Well, maybe it's time I filled you in on some inside information.

My home has two occupants—myself and a calico cat named Kid-Wid. Her strange name was adopted from a friend's cat that was no longer living. I thought the name was cute, and somehow it just seemed to fit.

To be honest, I'm not a big cat lover. I prefer dogs, but they aren't allowed in the condominium where I live. I do like cats that are sweet and affectionate, but in my experience, this type of temperament is extremely rare.

Maybe the problem is the type of cats I select. I've always been drawn to playful, frisky kittens that grow up to be independent, "don't-give-a-rip" adult critters. This description fits Kid-Wid to a tee. Over the years she and I have learned merely to tolerate one another. When I pick her up, she immediately meows to let me know she'd rather be back on the floor. When I place her in my lap, her body tenses and her ears go back, alerting me that she's plotting an escape. Clearly, the relationship between Kid-Wid and me is rocky. Every once in a while we connect emotionally, but these moments are rare.

One night several years ago, I was preparing to leave on a trip. I took Kid-Wid to a friend's house so he could care for her while I was away. As I was gathering her belongings from the car, I made the mistake of leaving her unattended. When I turned my back, she fled the scene. After seemingly endless searching, I became seriously concerned. The fact that my friend lived on a busy street corner only added to the anxiety.

I immediately began to pray and asked family members to do the same. The next day I combed the area, stopping every few minutes to call Kid-Wid's name and shake her food box. Frankly, I was surprised by my reaction. This was an animal that I hadn't been too fond of twenty-four hours before. Now I was on the verge of tears.

At ten o'clock that night, I spotted a familiar face peeking out from behind a bush. It was Kid-Wid! In typical fashion, she tried to run from me, but I caught her. I scooped her up in my arms and held her close.

"Thank you, God," I said with tears rolling down my cheeks. "Thank you for helping me find Kid-Wid."

I thought later about that incident and how it illustrated God's love for His undeserving children. If I could be so concerned for a cat that I didn't particularly like, how much more does our heavenly Father care for each of us? Remember the parable Jesus told about the shepherd who wouldn't rest until he found his lost sheep? That story speaks of the Lord's concern for each of His children. Even though we do stupid things and wander away from His protective care, He knows exactly where we are and urges us to "come home." Jesus "wants all men to be saved and to come to a knowledge of the truth" (1 Timothy 2:4).

Still, rebellion against the Shepherd is a dangerous thing. Just as Kid-Wid ran blindly at night on busy streets, we risk everything when we defy the guiding principles in the Bible. They are there to protect us from our willful spirits and the consequences that follow. King David said, "Thy rod and Thy staff, they comfort me" (Psalm 23:4, NASB). I once heard a sermon that was based on that Scripture. The pastor explained how a shepherd uses his staff to guard the flock. Because sheep are unintelligent creatures, they can easily encounter a dangerous situation. When a shepherd sees a sheep getting too close to the edge of a cliff, for example, he reaches out with his staff and hooks the animal across the chest. Then he pulls the sheep to safety.

What David meant in Psalm 23 is that we find comfort through the protection of our heavenly Father, the Great Shepherd. Even His discipline, although sometimes painful, is an expression of His love.

Well, Kid-Wid is back home these days and doing fine. You'll be pleased to know that the situation between this cranky cat and me is improving. She actually stayed on my lap for two minutes the other day—a record!

your turn

①

Is your relationship with Jesus Christ the best that it can be? If not, what are some ways that you can improve your relationship with Him?

②

Name an incident when the Shepherd protected you from going astray.

KEEP THE FAITH

Check It Out!
2 CORINTHIANS 5:7

Have you read the verse that says, "The just shall live by faith" (Galatians 3:11, KJV)? How about this one: "Faith comes by hearing, and hearing by the Word of God" (Romans 10:17, NKJV)? Or this one: "We walk by faith, not by sight" (2 Corinthians 5:7, NKJV)?

What do you think these passages mean? Well, one thing is obvious: Faith is very important to God! The Bible talks about faith as a willful decision to believe in Jesus Christ and the principles of Scripture, even when we lack concrete evidence or proof.

The Lord could have eliminated the need for faith altogether. He could have given us the ability to heal the sick and raise the dead. Jesus Himself could stand before us and hold a casual conversation in the afternoon. But those situations don't happen. Why? Because faith is important to God. He wants us to choose to believe—not to be forced, perhaps by fear, to accept the truth.

Have you ever concluded that God doesn't exist or that He is impersonal and doesn't care about you? Maybe this is where you're at right now. What do you think He wants of you at a moment like this? Let me suggest that you pray these words, expressed in Mark 9:24: "Lord, I believe; help my unbelief." He will grant greater faith to those who ask.

I'm reminded of a situation that happened to a friend, Amy, and her family. She and her parents were seated at a restaurant, talking about Jesus. Amy and her mom were new Christians, but her father hadn't accepted the message of the gospel. He was stubborn and full of disbelief.

As they sat there talking, Amy's dad became more frustrated. Finally, he blurted out, "If Jesus is everything that He claimed to be, then why doesn't He open the sky and reveal Himself to me?"

About that time, a poorly dressed man entered the restaurant selling postcards. He didn't approach any of the tables except the one where Amy and her parents were sitting. Without saying a word, he displayed the cards to them. Each one had a different spiritual image on the front.

Amy's parents thought the cards were pretty, so they bought three of them. The man nodded and left without stopping to sell cards to anyone else in the restaurant. It wasn't until after he was gone that Amy and her parents noticed the picture on one of the cards. They couldn't believe their eyes! It was a drawing of Jesus, with the sky open above Him and light streaming down.

Just five minutes earlier, Amy's dad had asked Jesus to open the sky and reveal Himself. Amy quickly jumped up from her chair and ran outside to see the man again, but he was gone.

Was that man an angel, a messenger from God? Perhaps. Regardless, I have no doubt that the Lord used him to convey His message of hope and faith to Amy's father. Why would He do that? Because He cares deeply about Amy's father, just as He loves you and me. I'm happy to say that it wasn't long after this experience that Amy's dad received Jesus as his Lord and Savior.

Isn't that an awesome story? If God would strengthen the faith of a doubting unbeliever, will He not also grant greater faith to those of us who already have a relationship with Him? I believe He will. All we have to do is pray and make the request.

Have you ever considered this question: If God knows what we need, why does He want us to ask Him and to walk by faith? The Scriptures say, "Your Father knows what you need before you ask him" (Matthew 6:8). Why then are our prayers necessary? The reason is that without prayer, there is no relationship. The Lord wants us to talk to Him and know Him personally. Just as you and your girlfriends must communicate to really know each other, we need to express in regular, sincere conversation our deep longings, our hopes, our fears, our regret over sin, our praise, and our love for the Lord. That's how we form a relational bond with Him.

Earlier today I sought the Lord's counsel about a decision. As I asked for guidance, a thought came to my mind that resolved the dilemma. I was given a plan of action. God doesn't always answer my prayers so quickly, but He works everything out for the best. This is how I know He's involved in my life.

Is He involved in your life? Can you see His hand at work in response to your prayers? Are you convinced of His love for you? If not, you may want to start immersing yourself in the Word and communicating with Him through prayer. That is the surest way to grow in your faith.

I like the analogy I once heard from a young boy: "Jesus is like the wind—you can't see Him or touch Him, but you know He's there."

And so He is for all of us—if we believe.

your turn

①

Are you convinced of everything the Bible teaches? Rate the intensity of your faith on a scale of 1-10 (with 10 being GREAT FAITH and 1 being NO FAITH).

②

Take some time to talk to the Lord about where you rated your faith. If you answered five or lower, then you need to do some faith-building exercises. Pump up your prayer life and the amount of time you spend reading God's Word. Sometimes it helps to find another person who is willing to pray and study with you. (No matter where you fit on the scale, there will always be an opportunity to grow closer to God. That's the beauty of having a relationship with Him; we are continuously being transformed into His likeness.)

CASH VALUE

Check It Out!
MATTHEW 6:24

Let's focus on a topic that interests everybody: money! You've heard that it has power and that it can "talk" and "make the world go 'round." But did you know that Jesus spoke about this subject more than any other? It's true! He referred to money more than He did heaven, hell, sin, repentance, love, or even His second coming. Why would Jesus concentrate so much on the dangers of money and materialism?

For the answer, consider the story in Matthew 19 of the rich young ruler. This wealthy man approached Jesus and revealed that he had been faithful in obeying the commandments. Then he asked, "What good thing must I do to get eternal life?" Jesus answered by saying, "If you want to be perfect, go, sell your possessions and give to the poor, and you will have treasure in heaven. Then come, follow me" (v. 21). The rich ruler walked away sad, because the price for him was literally too great to pay.

Why do you think Jesus asked the man to do such a difficult thing? The reason is that the man's possessions had become his god, and he would not part with them. He was unwilling to give up what was standing between him and the Lord. As Jesus said in Matthew 6:24, "No one can serve two masters. Either he will hate the one and love the other, or he will be devoted to the one and despise the other. You cannot serve both God and Money."

It is also true that those who hunger and thirst for great wealth are easily duped or enticed into making costly mistakes. As the Scriptures say, "People who want to get rich fall into temptation and a trap and into many foolish and harmful desires that plunge men into ruin and destruction" (1 Timothy 6:9).

Who comes to mind when you read this verse? I think of gamblers—people who are trying to "get rich quick." They hang out in casinos, buy lottery tickets, or use the Internet to try to hit the jackpot. Never mind the fact that these folks have a greater chance of getting struck by lightning than winning the big one—that doesn't stop them. In fact, someone playing the $325 million Big Game lottery is sixteen times more likely to be killed driving to the gas station to buy a ticket than to win the jackpot.[1] Sadly, many gamblers lose their savings and even their families as a result of this addiction.

But you don't have to be a gambling addict to be dazzled by what money has to offer. NBC television launched a game show hosted by Regis Philbin. The program was called *Who Wants to Be a Millionaire?* When the show first aired, the network was bowled over by the ratings success. It was an instant hit! Why? Because people are mesmerized by the appeal of easy money. The mere *possibility* was enough to hold the interest of TV viewers across the nation.

Does the Lord prohibit us from being rich? Is He against us buying new clothes, stereos, laptops, and cars? Certainly not. Wealth is not evil in and of itself. Abraham, David, and other great men of the Bible were blessed with riches. In fact, the Scriptures indicate that God gives some people the power to get wealthy (Deuteronomy 8:18 and 1 Samuel 2:7).

Then at what point does money become dangerous? The apostle Paul clarified for us that money is not the problem. It is the *love* of money that is the root of all evil (1 Timothy 6:10). We get into trouble when our possessions begin to possess us!

I'm reminded of a guy I knew in college who started a successful business. He was already wealthy by the age of twenty. One day

---

[1]Associated Press, "How Hard Is It to Win the Lottery?" *Daily Herald,* 16 April 2002.

he showed up at school in a brand-new red Porsche. The license plate read VIP TOYS. He and his girlfriend offered to take me for a ride in this "very important person's toy," so I hopped in the front seat and we sped off. As we glided down the highway, I complimented this young man on his new Porsche. I'll never forget his response. With some nonchalance he said, "Actually I'm going to sell it pretty soon and buy a Lamborghini—I want a car that performs better." I could tell that this guy would never be satisfied with his "toys," because materialism had taken control of his life.

As you can see, not only are there pitfalls for those who seek riches, but the few who acquire them are often disappointed. They quickly learn that wealth will not satisfy them or bring meaning to their lives. No amount of money will do that. There has to be a better reason for living than chasing after material items and big bank accounts.

Now that we've exposed the *wrong* approach toward money and possessions, let's talk about what's right. Some of you are familiar with the concept of tithing. This is when we give 10 percent (or more) of our income to the Lord. It is something that we as Christians are required to do, not because God needs our money, but because we need to give it. Sharing what we have keeps our priorities in order and our materialistic lusts in check. Also, by giving the Lord our "firstfruits," we are acknowledging that He has control of our finances.

Let's take it a step further. Some people believe that the buck stops with their tithe—that the Lord is entitled to 10 percent, but the other 90 percent belongs to them. Not true; God owns it all! "The earth is the Lord's, and everything in it, the world, and all who live in it" (Psalm 24:1). Everything we have is on loan from Him, and we are stewards of all He has entrusted to us. That means that your CDs, books, blue jeans, and jewelry are purchased with His money.

If you understand this concept, it becomes clear that every spending decision is a *spiritual* decision. If you waste food, for example, you are not squandering your own resources—you're squandering what belongs to the Lord. If you buy an excessive number of

DVDs in a year, you're not blowing your own cash—you're wasting what belongs to God. Everything is a gift from His hand.

Finally, remember that no matter how much money you acquire in a lifetime, you'll never have enough for all you would like to buy or do. Even billionaires have some limit on their purchasing power.

A few years ago a guy I know landed a fifty-thousand-dollar contract with a major corporation. He immediately began purchasing things that he wanted—a microwave, a new television set, an expensive car. Because his standard of living had increased, he needed to keep the cash coming in. Eventually, he found himself staring at the ceiling at night, trying to come up with ways to make his car payments and clear his credit-card bills.

Extravagance at one point will lead to frustration at another point. Good business managers keep the big picture in mind as they make their financial decisions.

So what's the bottom line? Let me sum it up in one simple sentence: *The secret to successful living is to spend your life on something that will last throughout eternity.* Achieving wealth and possessions is not a worthy objective. Or as someone once said, "You'll never see a U-Haul hooked up to the back of a hearse."

your turn

1

Why did Jesus ask the wealthy ruler to sell his possessions?

2

What can happen to people who want to get rich? (See 1 Timothy 6:9.)

3

Take a moment to reflect on your own financial priorities. What are your general feelings about money and personal wealth?

4

Do you tithe? Why is tithing important?

GOD IS COOL!

Check It Out!
PSALM 92:4-5

What does it mean to be "cool"? *Cool* is one slang word that's still used today. During its origin back in the 1960s, some other phrases meant about the same thing. *Groovy, right on,* and *far out* are pretty much out of date now, but *cool* has withstood the test of time.

When I was in high school, being cool meant that you dressed in style, had respectable friends, and never said anything ridiculous. In other words, you weren't a nerd.

My brother, Ryan, and I use the word *cool* to describe every thing from cars to movies. It's a reliable way to reveal how much we like something. If I say something is cool, that means it's extraordinary—at the top of my A-list.

Well, you know what? *God* is cool![2] In fact, He's so cool that there aren't enough words to describe Him! I know He's an awesome being to be feared and worshiped. His wrath can be a terrible thing (just skim the Old Testament). His power is infinite and we are always to honor Him in reverence. But when you get right down to it, He's also really cool. Who else could create a giraffe? What was He thinking when he made an aardvark? You can't look at a pig and tell me that God has no sense of humor.

---

[2]"God Is Cool!" is based on an article by Jerry Vallotton in *The Clause,* April 1984. Used with permission.

How about humans? Just the other day I was strolling through the mall, and I had a great opportunity to see the Lord's idea of variety. There were more flavors than you'd find at Baskin-Robbins! Tall, short, wide, thin—people of all different colors and races.

Snow is created by God, too. Who else could have thought of something you can ski on one day and drink the next? And how about water? We get to swim and splash around and jump off diving boards without breaking any bones!

Let's move on to food. One of my favorites is a watermelon—an event in itself. You put your whole face into it as the sweet juice runs down your neck, and then you get to spit out the seeds! Avocados are creative, too. They have their own little traveling case, and they taste great in guacamole (another weakness of mine).

How about falling in love? Now there's a concept! A boy and a girl get together, and WOW—tingles and heartbeats, sweaty palms, flowers, cards, walks in the moonlight, and holding hands. Super cool idea!

God is not boring. He's into excitement. Read the Bible, and you'll find more happenings than *Star Wars*, *Titanic,* and *The Wizard of Oz* put together! There are dragons in Job, a talking donkey in the book of Numbers, lions in Daniel, bears in 2 Kings, and giants all over the place. There are seas being split, water turning to wine, days being extended, blind guys seeing, dead men rising, and if that's not enough for you, just check out Revelation!

On a personal level, God is cool because He listens to our prayers and doesn't laugh (out loud at least). He understands what it's like to be human. He can relate to being made fun of or biting your tongue while eating lunch. He feels for us when we have pimples or drop salsa on our clean, white shirt. Why else would God write a book on how to live if He didn't understand how we operate? The Bible covers everything from depression to how to handle your finances.

Isn't it amazing that the Creator of the universe would desire a personal relationship with each of us? It's mind-boggling to comprehend why He would even care!

Maybe this is why I love Him so much. He makes me feel special even though I'm a little speck on this big planet. He makes me feel like "I'm the one."

Thanks, God, for being so cool!

your turn

①

Name some aspects about God that have special meaning for you.

②

Think of some ways that you can thank God for His creativity.

Let's talk about FAMILY!

Daddy's Girl But, Mom, Everybody's Wearing It!
Cool or Bizarre? It's My Life
Treasured Memories
Oh, Brother!

TREASURED
MEMORIES

Check It Out!
PROVERBS 10:7

We have lots of traditions in my family—things we do at least once a year that symbolize what we believe. I credit my mother for this. She has always held a strong belief that family togetherness should be a priority in every home. Awhile back, she put these thoughts on paper and cowrote a book entitled *Let's Make a Memory*. It is a collection of activities and traditions that we've enjoyed through the years—many of which my mother originated.

One of my favorite family traditions takes place on Thanksgiving day, right after the "feeding frenzy." We begin by giving everyone at the table two kernels of Indian corn. Then we pass a basket, and as we drop in the corn, we express two things for which we're thankful to God. We rarely get the basket around the table without a few tears! I remember sitting next to my dad one Thanksgiving when I was thirteen years old. As the basket was handed to him, he dropped in his corn and said with emotion, "I'm thankful for two people—Danae and Ryan." I was very touched by my father's expression of love for me and my brother. Even though this happened a long time ago, that memory has stayed with me ever since.

Another ritual that my mother started is our candlelight ceremony on Christmas Eve. After dimming the lights, we sit in a circle while my dad reads the Christmas story. No, I'm not referring to

'*Twas the Night before Christmas.* I'm talking about the story of Jesus' birth that's found in the second chapter of Luke.

After Dad closes the Bible, everyone is given a small, narrow candle to hold. We each take turns lighting our candles and sharing about the past year—the significant events that have taken place in our lives and what the Lord has taught us. We go on to reveal what we hope God will do in the new year, perhaps focusing on a spiritual goal. As each person finishes talking, he or she lights the next person's candle, and so it continues around the circle until all the candles are lit. We then blow out our candles, and Dad closes our time together with prayer.

I think our candlelight ceremony is especially important during the busy Christmas season. It forces us to take time to reflect upon Jesus, who is the Light of the World. I've actually started this tradition among my own circle of friends. For the past three Decembers, I've cooked a little dinner and followed the meal with a candlelight ceremony. My girlfriend Loreen likes this tradition so much that she started one in her own family.

What is the purpose of having traditions and making memories? Well, for one thing, it's fun! But the main reason for these activities is to help us understand who we are, what we believe, and what makes our family unique. If you've seen the movie *Fiddler on the Roof*, then you know that tradition is the theme of the story. In one of the first scenes, the main character, Tevye, sings about the importance of tradition in the Jewish culture. In the middle of the song, Tevye suddenly stops and says, "Why do we do these things? I don't know—but it's a TRADITION!" He goes on to say that his people have traditions for everything—how to sleep, how to eat, how to work, how to wear clothes. Tevye makes a profound statement when he says, "Because of our traditions, every one of us knows who he is and what God expects him to do."

Traditions perform a vital function in a family because they give us *identity*. We especially need that understanding of ourselves today! Our families are so harried and distracted that we often do not feel close. That's why we have to work harder to make sure there's a bonding and a uniqueness to our inner circle. Traditions are a way of saying, "This is what we believe and how we are different from everyone else."

Do you have traditions in your family? If not, why don't you start one or two? My guess is that your efforts will be well received. Your parents, grandparents, and siblings would probably welcome the opportunity for a candlelight ceremony. Perhaps you can talk to your mom about working together to develop some fun and meaningful activities. For example, if your family members are Christians, you might suggest making brunch and having devotions together on Saturday mornings.

My girlfriend Loreen doesn't wait for her parents to plan activities—she does it on her own (with their permission, of course). She sets up board-game nights with pizza and plans a picnic on the Fourth of July. Loreen obviously understands the importance of investing in the lives of her family. To her, the time and preparation is minimal compared to the lifelong memories that are made.

Proverbs 10:7 (NASB) says, "The memory of the righteous is blessed." Think about that verse for a moment. What does it mean to you? For myself, I define it in a personal way. I remember my grandmother, now deceased, who demonstrated her love by making all of our holidays special. I can still see her smiling face and taste the wonderful southern dishes that she prepared. Her memory is a blessing to me. As I think back to my childhood, I remember how my mom took the time to start a neighborhood Bible study for me and about ten other kids during the summer. With a loving spirit, she served refreshments and used Bible stories to teach us about Jesus. That memory is a blessing to me. I think of my dad, who found the energy after a hard day's work to wrestle on the floor with Ryan and me and read us a bedtime story. Those memories are also a blessing to me.

Who has been a blessing in *your* life? Who has left a lasting impression upon you?

All of us need to feel that we're not just part of a cluster of people existing together in a house, but we're a *family*—a family that is conscious of its own character, uniqueness, and heritage. That special relationship of love and companionship "glues" us together with identity and personality. It makes us extremely valuable to one another.

Why not thank God now for any special memories you've enjoyed in your home? Then think of some traditions you'd like to start, and pray that they will help to draw your family closer to each other and to the Lord. That's a good way to invest in the lives of those you love the most.

your turn

❶
Why are family traditions important?

❷
What are some traditions/activities you could start to help you and your family grow spiritually?

DADDY'S GIRL

Check It Out!
DEUTERONOMY 5:16

"Higher, Daddy!" I squealed as my thirty-five-pound body dropped into his outstretched hands. Once again, my father hurled me to the clouds (at least it felt that high), and I giggled all the way down. For an energetic three-year-old, this was just about the biggest thrill ever. I wanted Daddy to repeat the "air-toss" game again and again.

On the weekends, he took me for bicycle rides. I had my own little seat on the back of his ten-speed. We would glide down the road with the sun on our backs and the wind in our faces, often stopping at our favorite fast-food place, Taco Lita. On other days, we would get ice-cream cones and ride to the park. While we were there, my dad would push me in the swing and build a sand castle with me. Our creations always looked realistic—never a lopsided mess with a flag stuck on top. Each one had a drawbridge and a moat, just like the real thing. Part of the fun was filling and refilling those moats with water!

My father was very busy while I was growing up, but he always had time for his little girl. At home, I used to crawl behind him while he was working at his desk. He never pushed me away or told me to find something to do. My presence was always appreciated. Every now and then, he would take a break to wrestle on the floor or play a game with me.

Dad was a master at getting in touch with my imagination (probably a result of his Ph.D. in child development!). He and I used to crawl underneath the covers of my parents' king-size bed and pretend that we were in a cave. Outside the "cave" there were bears and the weather was cold. As long as we stayed inside our refuge, we would be safe and warm. I would crawl to the top of the covers and peek out to make sure there were no bears in sight. Then I would quickly slide back into the "cave" for safety. What a fun experience that was!

Of course, not all my childhood memories are pleasant. There were conflicts and spankings. (Note: My dad was not one to "spare the rod." In fact, he wrote the best-selling book *Dare to Discipline*.) As I entered my teen years, my father and I sometimes locked horns over rules and curfews and money. Even though we didn't always see eye to eye, it never hindered our love for each other. The bond between us remained strong and true.

Throughout my life, my dad has always been there for me—sometimes when I wasn't even expecting it. A long time ago, I had a terrible fight with a boyfriend, and I was very upset. I can remember standing in front of the window, crying my eyes out. I thought I was alone. All of a sudden, I felt two hands on my shoulders. I whirled around to see my dad standing there. He put his arms around me and held me close as I sobbed into his shirt. Neither one of us said a word. Later, he and my mom and I talked the conflict out in detail. I felt so much better afterwards.

That experience reemphasized what I already knew to be true: Friends and boyfriends may come and go, but my dad will always be there for me.

We still share a special relationship. As I'm writing this, we're in Palm Desert, California, completing our individual projects. My dad is writing in one room and I'm in another. In between the working hours, we've enjoyed some good laughs, wonderful food, and interesting movies. Our love of history has prompted us to watch video documentaries together on ancient Rome, the American Revolution, and Napoleon's Battle of Waterloo. Okay—and yes, we've done Blockbuster, too!

A few years ago, Dad suffered a stroke which, thank the Lord, left no lasting effects. It did, however, make me more appreciative of every day that I have with him. I look for opportunities to put my arms around his neck and tell him I love him—to express how happy I am to be his daughter. Every day is a gift from God, and I'm so grateful that He's given me more time to spend with my father. It's a privilege that I thank the Lord for regularly!

How is your relationship with *your* father? Is it healthy, or is it marred by tension and conflict? If it's not good, I hope that you'll work at improving the communication lines. Remember what I said about making the most of every day—I wish someone had convinced me of that during my "independent stage." I would have reconsidered some of my words and actions.

Right now, some of you may be thinking, "It's easy for you to offer that advice, Danae, but you don't know *my* father! He's abusive! He's an alcoholic! I've never even heard him say that he loves me!"

I realize that there are many dads out there who haven't earned the title. It may seem impossible to reach out to a parent who has done little or nothing to deserve your affection. Why even bother to try?

As with all of life's conflicts, we need to look to God's Word for guidance. The fifth commandment is found in Deuteronomy 5:16. It reads, "Honor your father and your mother." Notice that the words are direct and to the point—no clauses or exceptions. I believe that the Lord wants us to follow this command, even if we don't think our parent(s) deserves honor.

What does it mean to honor someone? One dictionary defines it this way: "To hold in high respect." Does God actually expect us to show respect to a "deadbeat dad" who's never around? Yes, He does! By requiring us to have a loving attitude toward our parents (and toward all people), the Lord is protecting us from anger, resentment, and bitterness that can destroy us from within. It is His plan for the entire human family to "love one another."

Remember, too, that the respect you give to your dad might be the one thing that will soften his heart. I know that it's difficult to reach out to a parent when every fiber of your being screams, "No way!" But this is what Jesus wants you to do. With His help, you can forgive your dad for the pain he has caused you. If you haven't done so already, start praying about this! God will provide you with the direction to begin the healing process. Who knows? You might be instrumental in strengthening your dad's relationship with the Lord!

For those of you who don't have a dad in your life, I have some good news for you: Your heavenly Father loves you more than you could ever comprehend. If you are His child, He will always give you the guidance and support you need. Hosea 14:3 sums it up in a beautiful way: "In you the fatherless find compassion." What a comforting promise!

In a sense, I guess every one of us is a "Daddy's girl"—safe and secure in the love of our heavenly Father. I really like that feeling, don't you?

your turn

①

What are the three best aspects about your relationship with your dad? For example, do you spend time together? Does he teach you about life and God?

②

What are three areas that need improvement? (You may want to discuss these with your father so that you can work on them together.)

③

Can you think of some ways you can show love to your dad this week?

"He will turn the hearts of the fathers to their children, and the hearts of the children to their fathers."

MALACHI 4:6

OH, BROTHER!

Check It Out!
ROMANS 15:5-7

Okay, so they break your stuff, get on your nerves, and borrow your CDs without asking. Could anyone annoy you more than your brothers and sisters (or, to use the more technical term, *siblings*)?

Sure, you love them, but there are days when you wish they would disappear. What is it about living under the same roof with other kids that can be such a challenge?

I have only one sibling—a younger brother—but that didn't put me at an advantage. Like most siblings, Ryan and I had our share of squabbles. Sometimes I teased him too much; sometimes he was grouchy and irritable with me. There were days when we needed a break from each other.

Ryan and I are great friends now, but when I look back on my growing-up years, I recall moments when I should have been a better big sister. I didn't *always* fail in that regard, but I could have been a little less selfish and a little more loving. I'm thinking in particular about how I used to hog food. When Mom would buy a cereal variety pack, I would try to eat the Cocoa Krispies, Corn Pops, and Froot Loops before Ryan could get to them. Then there was the issue of controlling the television remote. Ryan and I got into some hefty disputes over that.

The other day I stumbled across a passage in Scripture that is relevant to sibling rivalry. Romans 15:5-7 says, "May the God who gives endurance and encouragement give you a spirit of unity among yourselves as you follow Christ Jesus, so that with one heart and mouth you may glorify the God and Father of our Lord Jesus Christ. Accept one another, then, just as Christ accepted you, in order to bring praise to God."

Would you say your relationship with your brothers and sisters is harmonious? According to this Scripture, it should be. This passage doesn't say occasional "tiffs" are acceptable. True, we all have diverse personalities that are bound to clash sometimes, but we should do our best to avoid this.

Most people don't realize that we're only afforded a small window of time to live with the family we're born into. At about eighteen years of age, most of us will move out and spread our wings. Life as we know it will never be the same again. That's why it's important to be a positive role model for our brothers and sisters while we can.

Are you aware that you're setting an example for your own siblings right now? You may not realize it, but your words and actions are being carefully monitored. I found this out when my brother submitted a school assignment for language class in sixth grade. I have the original paper framed and hanging in my condominium—spelling errors and all! This is what he wrote:

One of the Strongest Influences of My Life

My sister has been a great influence in my life. She has guied [guided] me since I was about three years old, in homework and Christ, etc. I know she will allways help me and protect me like she has in the past. Now I am older and can take care of myself, but she will allways answer questions. I love her very much and allways will. She is my best friend. Some day I will help her in any way that I can beause she has helped me in so many wase. I love her. The end.

By Ryan Dobson

Isn't that a nice compliment? I had no idea I was having such a positive influence on my little brother. I wasn't *striving* to teach him anything, but my everyday living was sending a message to him.

It doesn't matter if you're the youngest or the oldest; you can have a similar impact on your own siblings. When my grandfather was a teenager, his younger brother led him to Christ. That's a good example of how God can use your influence, regardless of your position in the family.

Those are just a few good reasons for "keeping the peace" with your siblings. Some of you are already getting along great, but others could stand to work on it. If you need help, start by calling on the Lord for guidance. Remember the invitation in Romans 15:5: "May the God who gives endurance and encouragement give you a spirit of unity among yourselves as you follow Christ Jesus." He will help you to experience joy in your family and create healthy relationships that will last a lifetime.

your turn

❶
Think of three ways you can improve your relationship with your sibling(s).

❷
What is one form of kindness you can practice this week?

❸
Test your brotherly (or sisterly) love by taking this quiz:

A. Your sister walks into your bedroom without knocking, and she *knows* the rules!
   - Your natural reaction is to _____.
   - Instead, you _____.
B. Your brother accidentally steps on your curling iron and breaks it.
   - Your natural reaction is to _____.
   - Instead, you _____.
C. Your sister borrows your favorite jacket and loses it at school.
   - Your natural reaction is to _____.
   - Instead, you _____.
D. Your brother carelessly forgets to give you the message that "Mr. Wonderful" called.
   - Your natural reaction is to _____.
   - Instead, you _____.

GOOD OL' DAYS

Check It Out!
PSALM 103:17-18

Let me ask you a question: If you are fortunate enough to have grandparents, do you spend much time with them?

I love getting together with mine! Although I lost one set of grandparents when I was young, my mom's folks are still alive and living close by. One of my favorite pastimes is driving to their house on Sunday afternoons for a visit. We spend the day eating, playing games, and sharing some good laughs. It's a special treat for me, especially since my mom and dad live a thousand miles away!

Now that I'm grown, I treasure the days spent with Grandma and Grandpa. There was a time when I didn't always appreciate that blessing. When I was in junior high, my grandparents would come and stay with my brother and me while my parents were out of town. Back then, I had a crush on a guy who lived across the street. I can still remember sliding down in the backseat of my grandparents' car when we'd drive past his house. I knew it was a silly thing to do, but I didn't want to come off looking childish in front of a cute guy. When you're in junior high, image is everything! Riding in an ancient Oldsmobile with my grandparents embarrassed me.

As I went through high school and college, I loved seeing Grandma and Grandpa at family gatherings, but I never took the initiative to visit them on my own. It wasn't as though I deliberately avoided them, but my priorities were with my friends. Then one night I rented an old movie called *Peggy Sue Got Married*. In the film, the main character, Peggy, went through a difficult time during her engagement. She began to reminisce about happier days and found herself thinking about her grandparents. The memories prompted her to drive to their house, where she received the comfort she was seeking.

That scene had a big impact on me! I thought of my own grandparents and all the happy memories we'd shared—little things like picking blackberries in their backyard, hearing stories about our family history, and the smell of Grandma's kitchen. It all took on a new meaning for me. I also wrestled with the fact that they lived just forty-five minutes away, yet I never went to see them. From that moment, I began to reprioritize my time so that I could visit them regularly. I'm happy to say that I've kept my resolution all these years, and it has been a joy.

Psalm 103:17-18 says, "From everlasting to everlasting the Lord's love is with those who fear him, and his righteousness with their children's children—with those who keep his covenant and remember to obey his precepts."

So true! A godly heritage can continue to live on from generation to generation. A friend of mine whose grandfather died last year just lost her grandmother three days ago. Though her grandparents have gone to heaven, they left a Christian legacy that has been passed down through three generations and now influences my friend and her five children.

Having a godly grandparent can impact you forever! As I mentioned earlier, my paternal grandfather passed away when I was young (twelve, to be exact), but the impression he left on me will never fade away. An evangelist, he took his relationship with Jesus Christ and his prayer life very seriously. During his first pastorate as a young man, he was known by his friends as the man with no leather on the toes of his shoes. That was because he spent so much time on his knees in prayer that the front of his shoes wore out before the soles did! How's that for spiritual heritage? When he died, there were two words engraved on his tombstone: *He prayed.* That epitaph pretty much summed up his life.

What can happen when a spiritual heritage is nonexistent? Last year my family and I traveled to Branson, Missouri, during spring break. While we were there, we went to an amusement park called Silver Dollar City. We had a great time going on rides and taking in shows. During one of the entertainment productions, I noticed a man and woman standing behind me. They appeared to be in their late fifties, and they were both wearing T-shirts with a picture of rapper Eminem's face on the front.

That's odd, I thought to myself. *Why would a couple at their age be into Eminem?*

I had to get to the bottom of it, so I turned to them and asked, "You like Eminem?"

"Yes," answered the man. "He's our grandson."

"We're very proud of him," the woman added, "so we wanted to wear these T-shirts today."

I chatted with them for a minute before introducing my dad, who seemed taken aback when he heard the rapper's name in connection with the couple.

After we said good-bye to them and parted ways, my dad and I reflected on the situation. We talked about how Eminem is known for his obscene lyrics and curse words, yet his grandmother said that she and his grandfather were proud of him. Why? And what did that comment say about their values?

Of course, I don't know them, but I wonder if there was ever a time when they had tried to pass on a Christian heritage to their grandson. When he was small, did they pray with him? Teach him about Jesus? Take him to church? Did they instill within him a love for God's Word and its principles? From what I know about Eminem's rap music, I can't see any evidence of a spiritual upbringing. Either his family doesn't know the Lord or he rejected what he learned.

Although Eminem is foul and hardened, not everyone who lacks a godly heritage will turn out this way. The Lord can do a tremendous work in anyone's life, regardless of the person's up-bringing or background. He could even save Eminem!

I'm sure that some of you have grandparents who aren't believers in Jesus. If that's the case, then remember to pray for their salvation. It's never too late! Regardless, try to increase the amount of time you spend with them. I realize not everyone is within driving distance, and some of you don't even have a driver's license yet, but we all have access to a telephone! If you're not doing it already, why not set a goal to make contact every other week? It would mean the world to your grandparents, and you'll find it rewarding, too.

your turn

①
What are some characteristics about your grandparents that you admire?

②
Name a contribution that each of your grandparents has made to your life.

③
Think of something kind to do this week to demonstrate your love for your grandparents.

"Rise in the presence of the aged, show respect for the elderly and revere your God."

LEVITICUS 19:32

FAMILY FEUD

Check It Out!
COLOSSIANS 3:12-14

I'm sure you've noticed that human beings are flawed and imperfect creatures. Every one of us has a tendency to be selfish, dishonest, and devious at times. The Scripture acknowledges this important aspect of our nature when it declares, "All have sinned and fall short of the glory of God" (Romans 3:23).

King David wrote, "I was sinful . . . from the time my mother conceived me" (Psalm 51:5). In other words, each of us has inherited a sinful nature that creeps into our thoughts, our motives, and our relationships with others. That is why we need a Savior who was and is perfect. Jesus Christ died as a sacrifice for the sins of those who repent and believe in His name. Then He conquered death by rising from the grave. This is the essence of the Christian faith.

Now let me take that understanding a step further. Because people are imperfect, it is invariably true that families are also flawed. Some are terribly destructive and unhealthy—called "dysfunctional" by therapists. Others are wonderfully loving, secure, and dedicated to each member. Even in the very best of families, however, conflict and misunderstanding are common. Parents can be at fault just as much as their children. We all irritate each other and sometimes hurt those we love the most. That is why we need to learn how to handle conflict and reduce the tensions when nerves are set on edge. Those times *will* come for all of us, and we should get ourselves ready for them.

I am fortunate to have been raised in a very loving and secure family. My brother, Ryan, and I were given the best care and nurturing. We, too, had our moments, though. I will never forget one such occasion that has come to be known in our family as "Black Sunday."

I was about ten years old at the time and Ryan was five. On this Sunday morning, the entire Dobson household overslept. What followed was an attempt to beat the clock as four irritable people scurried to get ready for church. Of course, my brother was dressed before the rest of us, enabling him to slip out the back door to play. Fifteen minutes later he reemerged with dirt stains on his "Sunday best." This necessitated a complete change of clothes, which infuriated my mother. The next thirty minutes were far from tranquil—a spanking was delivered, my dad accidently smeared black shoe polish on the carpet, and the milk went over the edge of the table! By the time we got to church, everyone's nerves were shot, and we couldn't have cared less about the sermon. In the words of my mother, "There wasn't a pastor in the world who could have moved us!"

That evening the four of us gathered in the family room for a "powwow." Ryan was given the first opportunity to vent, and he turned his frustration toward Mom. "You've been really grouchy today," he said. "And you've blamed me for everything all day long!" My mother then explained why she had been unhappy with him and apologized for overreacting.

Then it was my turn to blow off some steam. Finally, Mom and Dad expressed their own feelings about the day's conflicts. It was a valuable time of healing for our family as we poured out our discontentment and sought forgiveness from each other. Afterward, we prayed and asked the Lord to help us live and work together in love and harmony.

Have you and those you love experienced your own "Black Sunday"? Most families have times when rules are broken and the Christian principles by which they live are violated. It's easy to blame the kids, but parents, too, become tired and irritable, sometimes exploding over trivial matters. Right now some of you are probably thinking, *I know—tell me about it!* We all are capable of having a short fuse, and it doesn't take much to ignite it. This is understandable, but the important question is, What's the best way to reestablish friendship within your family *after* the storm has passed?

As I previously illustrated, one way to go about this is through nonthreatening, open communication. During the times when you and your family are at odds, why not sit down together and hash it out? In a respectful way, express your dissatisfaction and give everyone else a chance to do the same. Don't forget to invite the Lord to be at the center of your discussion (assuming your family members are Christians). You've probably heard the saying "The family that prays together, stays together." This is not just a catchy phrase on a bumper sticker—it's the truth! Miracles can occur when God is given the opportunity to work.

However, don't expect a supernatural miracle to fix your short fuse or brighten your brother's bad mood. God provides the Bible as the manual for maintaining harmony in the home. Here's a recipe for "peace in the family" that's found in Colossians 3:12-14:

> Therefore, as God's chosen people, holy and dearly loved, clothe yourselves with compassion, kindness, humility, gentleness and patience. Bear with each other and forgive whatever grievances you may have against one another. Forgive as the Lord forgave you. And over all these virtues put on love, which binds them all together in perfect unity.

What great words of truth! On a side note, isn't it amazing how God's Word touches on so many of our modern-day struggles? The timeless wisdom of the Scriptures is relevant to every dilemma we face.

In keeping with Colossians 3:12-14, I hope that you'll display some kindness and compassion toward your mom and dad, even on days when you wish you could be free of their rules and authority. If you're like most young people, you'd prefer to have total independence, but you're probably not ready for such liberation.

You may even have a distinct set of "rules" that you expect your parents to understand. Being cool and using your own lingo is a big one. If Mom and Dad can't relate to the latest slang word that's not in the dictionary, oh well! Privacy is also a necessity—can you ever get enough of it? Then there's the desire to wear certain hairstyles and fashions (purses and shoes included) that parents sometimes find objectionable. Finally, in a social setting among peers, most teens would prefer that Mom and Dad keep their distance.

All of these "idiosyncrasies" can drive the average parent to the loony farm! Okay, not really, but is it any wonder they sometimes say and do things they regret?

I now can sympathize with my parents in regard to what they went through during my adolescent years. If I had to do it over again, I'd probably be a little more understanding of the "parental perspective."

Most moms and dads are trying to do their God-given job to the best of their ability. They may make mistakes along the way, but they are trying to do what is right. So give them a break! Someday you'll want your own children to do the same—especially on a "Black Sunday."

your turn

①

Think of a time when you thought your mom or dad made a "parental goof." How did you respond?

②

Does your family go through periods where everyone is grouchy and short-tempered? What is an effective approach to getting back on track?

③

How often do you pray for your mom and dad? Have you considered asking God to give them wisdom in relating to you? Now there's a thought!

SEVENTY TIMES SEVEN

Check It Out!
MATTHEW 18:22

I was talking with a friend the other day (I'll call him Bryan), and he shared some details about his past with me.

When Bryan was six years old, his parents sat down with the family and announced they were getting a divorce. Bryan later found out that it was his mother's decision, and that she was leaving his dad for another man. She moved out shortly thereafter and left Bryan and his two siblings with their father. It was a painful experience for the entire family.

To make matters worse, Bryan's mother would often make plans to get together with him and then forget to pick him up. He would wait for hours with his tote bag by the door, but she'd never arrive. When it got to be nine or ten o'clock at night, he'd call his mom, and she'd say that she had forgotten and offer to pick him up in the morning. This experience always left him feeling hurt and disappointed—in his words, "like chopped liver."

After Bryan relayed this sad story to me, he went on to say something profound. He told me that even though the memories are still there, he hardly ever thinks about them anymore. He now has a good relationship with his mom, and he doesn't hold a grudge against her for the pain that she caused. In fact, he prays regularly for her salvation (his mother is not a Christian), and he drives an hour to visit her on Sunday afternoons. I asked Bryan how he was able to get past the disappointment, especially since his mother has never cleaned up her act.

"Oh, I forgave her a long time ago," Bryan replied.

"Did she *ask* for your forgiveness?"

"No," he said. "It was a decision I made in my own heart."

Bryan's testimony had an impact on me. It showed how the Lord can help someone heal and get beyond a grievous offense.

Like Bryan, all of us have wounds that have been inflicted on us through the years. Many hurtful situations occur within our own families. Some of us come from broken homes or abusive backgrounds. Others never knew their dad or mom and grew up feeling unwanted or unloved. Even in Christian homes, the pain can be great. How are we supposed to forgive people who don't deserve it and, in some cases, don't even care?

The Scriptures are loaded with verses that speak about this subject. Jesus Himself taught the importance of forgiveness on numerous occasions. At one point, His disciple Peter approached Him and asked, "Lord, how many times shall I forgive my brother when he sins against me? Up to seven times?"

Jesus said to him, "I do not say to you, up to seven times, but up to seventy times seven" (Matthew 18:22, NASB).

Jesus went on to tell a story about a servant who owed his master a very large sum of money. The servant was unable to pay, so his master ordered him to sell everything he had to cover the debt. The penalty included a sentence of slavery for himself and his family. Upon hearing this, the servant fell to his knees and begged for mercy. His master took pity on him and in compassion canceled the debt and let him go free.

Afterwards, the servant came upon a fellow servant who owed him a small amount of money. The first man grabbed the fellow servant and began to choke him, saying, "Pay back what you owe me!"

The servant dropped to his knees and begged for mercy. He pleaded for some time to pay back the debt, but the first servant refused and had him thrown into prison. When this news reached the master, he was very angry. He called the first servant in and said, "You wicked servant! . . . I canceled all that debt of yours because you begged me to. Shouldn't you have had mercy on your fellow servant just as I had on you?" (32-33). In anger his master had him thrown in jail until he could pay back all that he owed.

Jesus concluded by saying, "This is how my heavenly Father will treat each of you unless you forgive your brother from your heart" (Matthew 18:35).

All of us owe the Lord a tremendous debt because of our sins. It's an amount that we're held accountable for but are unable to pay. The wonderful news is that when we humbly confess our sins and ask for forgiveness, we are *released* from that debt. God, in His great compassion and mercy, cancels what we owe and sets us free! Isn't that an amazing act of love?

Do you see why we ought to forgive one another as we have been forgiven? No one will ever sin against you as much as you have sinned against God. If He has canceled your enormous debt, shouldn't you forgive the smaller debt of the person who has offended you? To do so is to please the Lord and to honor Him.

There is another important payoff that comes with forgiveness: We set ourselves free from our own "prison." You see, when we don't forgive someone, we become slaves to anger and bitterness. It affects the way we think, the way we sleep, our appetites, our relationship with God and other people, and even our own personalities. We get stuck in a rut, while bitterness, like a cancer, eats away at our soul. The result is pure misery!

Have you experienced this in your own life? Perhaps there was someone you stayed mad at for a long time. Did your emotions control your thoughts and behavior? Personally, I know there have been times when I was eager to settle the score or put an end to a friendship. My bad attitude did nothing to help me heal. Instead, I became completely miserable—walking around feeling sorry for myself and seeking revenge on my offender. It was only when I forgave that person and turned the matter over to the Lord that I was able to move on.

Some of you have been severely wounded in your lifetime. Maybe you've been physically abused or even raped. In some cases, it happened at the hands of a family member whom you trusted. The pain is so great that you don't think you'll ever be able to heal, and you certainly can't forgive him for what he has done.

My advice? Release it! Let it go. Give your burden to God and set yourself free from the bondage of a bitter heart. I like my pastor's description. He suggests that you put your offender(s) in the "Jesus Jail" and let Him deal with that person. It will only be after you have taken this step that you can truly begin to heal.

Keep in mind that forgiveness is not about saying that what your offender did was okay or giving that person your trust again if he or she hasn't changed. Forgiveness is also not about pretending you don't have a right to feel angry. Denial won't produce any long-term benefits.

So what is forgiveness? Let me end with a neat definition, provided by psychologist and author Dr. Archibald Hart. He said, "Forgiveness is giving up my right to hurt you for hurting me." That is precisely on target! Someone like Bryan who has been wounded by another person feels entitled to strike back—to retaliate. Something inside us demands revenge, but that is not the response Jesus taught. He wants us to surrender that "right" to hate in return. It is not easy to do, and, in fact, you *can't* do it on your own strength. But Jesus has promised to "forgive us our debts, as we also have forgiven our debtors" (Matthew 6:12).

Now, can you think of anyone *you* need to forgive?

your turn

❶

If someone has hurt you and does not ask for your forgiveness, what should you do?

❷

Jesus taught that we are to forgive from our heart. What does this mean to you?

Check It Out!

JAMES 3:17-18

It was five o'clock on a school night when the doorbell rang. I peeked through the shutters to see who it was. Cindy Mitchell, one of my sixth-grade classmates, was standing on the porch with her notebook and folder. When I opened the door, I could tell she'd been crying.

"Cindy!" I exclaimed. "What's wrong?"

"My mom and I got into an argument at the mall," she said, sniffing. "I told her I was leaving and that I wasn't coming back."

My mouth dropped open. "You mean you left your mom at the mall and walked a mile over here?" I asked.

Cindy nodded. "I got my homework out of the car on the way—I was hoping I could stay here awhile."

"Sure," I said, opening the door a little wider. "Come on in."

I knew right away that this situation was way over my head and that I'd better get my *own* mother involved. I brought Cindy into the family room and poured her a glass of iced tea. Through short breaths, she explained the fiasco to my mom. Fortunately, my mother has a gift for consoling and confronting at the same time. She encouraged Cindy to call her mom, and before long a frazzled woman arrived to pick up her daughter. Of course, by that time Cindy had calmed down and was content to go home.

I remember finding this event rather shocking. How could a

twelve-year-old get so angry that she'd run away? As I got older, I began to understand those feelings. No, I never took off, but there were moments during my teen years when I locked horns with my parents. Curfews and financial matters were often a source of conflict. What is it about adolescence that can create tension between those who love each other?

A lot of experts believe that the problem often results from the desire for power. More specifically, it has to do with control—control of others, control of our circumstances, and especially control of ourselves. The determination to have control lies deep within the human spirit. We all want to make our own decisions and run our own lives. Even toddlers strive for independence, throwing tantrums and going limp at the toy store when it's time to leave.

The grab for control is what produces most of the fights between parents and teenagers. Many adolescents are not content to receive their independence gradually. They want it yesterday. Mom and Dad are placed in a difficult position when this occurs. They have the God-given responsibility to lead their teens, but they can't force them to comply. The situation can result in a flurry of conflict.

I remember hearing about a girl who had an interesting way of giving her parents a message: After an emotional blowup, she would slam her bedroom door and blast the Billy Joel song "It's My Life." The tune's theme basically says, "Get lost and leave me alone." Frankly, I'm surprised this girl had access to her stereo after a tantrum like that—I probably would have lost the privilege.

Speaking of songs with independent themes, I've heard a couple of Britney Spears's tunes that carried this message, too. I'm thinking in particular of "I'm Not a Girl, Not Yet a Woman" and "Overprotected"—two songs that have a "Get lost and leave me alone" theme. As long as there are teenagers on this planet, there will always be pop music with lyrics about independence and control.

Okay, so perhaps you haven't been able to relate to anything I've written so far. You're one of those easygoing types who rarely has a run-in with your folks. If you are, then I applaud you. I hope you can breeze through adolescence with as little conflict as possible. But if you're like most teens, you're bound to clash with your parents on occasion. Maybe it will be in regard to what you wear or a broken curfew or a friend they disapprove of. When the confrontation occurs, how can you keep your cool and promote peace in your family?

Let's look at Scripture for advice. James 3:17-18 says, "The wisdom that comes from heaven is first of all pure; then peace-loving, considerate, submissive, full of mercy and good fruit, impartial and sincere. Peacemakers who sow in peace raise a harvest of righteousness."

What great truths these are. If we all lived by them, the world would be a much better place to live. Unfortunately, it's easier to read this passage than live by it. None of us is perfect, and conflicts are inevitable. But God can help us conquer our frustrations in a way that doesn't wound or damage.

If you're having a tough time getting along with your folks, remember that circumstances will not always stay the way they are. You won't always have to struggle to rid yourself of their authority. Your independence will be handed to you. Even five more years will bring remarkable changes in your relationship with them. With this in mind, I urge you to be charitable to your mom and dad. Sure, they may nag you about your messy room and your loud music and the amount of junk food you eat. They're *parents!* But the Bible speaks of a personal reward when you treat them well. "'Honor your father and mother'—which is the first commandment with a promise—'that it may go well with you and that you may enjoy long life on the earth'" (Ephesians 6:2-3).

So try to be a peacemaker in your family. You don't want to go through life with regrets over things you've said or done during these last years at home. No conflict is worth creating bitter memories that will linger into your adult life.

Some of you may have a good reason to be angry at your parents. But remember that you'll only be living at home with them for a few more years. Can you find it in your heart to forgive? Ask the Lord to help you, and He will.

God wants to enable you to build a relationship with your mom and dad that's free from anger and resentment. Isn't that what you want, too?

your turn

①
What is the biggest source of tension between you and your parents? How can you improve it?

②
How does God help us to become peacemakers? What eight traits will we exhibit if we have "the wisdom that comes from heaven"? (See James 3:17-18.)

③
Think of one way you can show love to each of your parents this week.

BUT, MOM! EVERYBODY'S WEARING IT!

Check It Out!
MATTHEW 6.28-30

It's common knowledge that keeping up with trends is important in school—especially junior high and beyond. Anyone who dresses weird or wears "wanna-be" labels might have a difficult time fitting in. If you're between seventh and twelfth grade, you know exactly what I'm talking about.

When you're in an atmosphere that's so focused on trends, it can be a bit strange to come home to your mom's matronly dresses or your dad's old-fashioned shoes.

Let's face it—most parents seem a little out of touch when it comes to current teen fads. They're never going to totally understand the lingo you use, the music you like, or the clothes you prefer. Chances are you'll never figure out their tastes, either. That is what's often referred to as the generation gap, and one day you'll probably experience it with your own children. Can you imagine a time when your kids will chuckle or roll their eyes when you mention 'N SYNC or Britney Spears? I trust me—that day is coming.

Not long ago an elderly lady who lives in the condominium beneath mine was blaring Frank Sinatra music. I smiled as the song "Young at Heart" drifted up through the floor. *Definitely a symbol of her generation,* I thought. *Few young people would be blasting Frank Sinatra on their stereo.*

There will always be changes in culture. That's why the latest fad is called "popular" or "pop." What's big news today will be history tomorrow. Each age group has a certain vibe that only they appreciate. So what's one way that we can close the generation gap? By respecting one another! Paul said it best in Romans 15:7: "Accept one another, then, just as Christ accepted you, in order to bring praise to God."

That can be difficult sometimes. I recall one Fourth of July when my parents threw a backyard barbecue. They invited ten couples and their kids to join in the fun. Before the event, Dad strolled into the kitchen sporting a pair of plaid Bermudas and some burgundy and gold U.S.C. tube socks.

"You're not actually going to wear that," I remarked.

"Sure I am," my father replied. "What's wrong with it?"

Fortunately, my mom sided with me, and together we convinced Dad to head back into the bedroom for a wardrobe change. To this day, it's still a mystery why Dad put on the bizarre outfit to begin with. Perhaps he did it for shock value—to provoke a reaction. Whatever the reason, I'm happy to report that it only happened once. My father usually dresses pretty spiffy!

Of course, he could easily point a finger at me, too. During my freshman year of college, I wore fingerless lace gloves and hair bows like Madonna, and my dad thought I was nuts!

I'm sure your parents are trying to make sense out of *your* wacky preferences. They're probably good sports about your music and that certain brand of jeans or sneaks you *must* have. If they aren't supportive, then it's probably for a good reason. Maybe an article of clothing you want is expensive—or perhaps it's unflattering or provocative.

Recently, some boys that I know went school-clothes shopping with their mom. She took them to a store called TJ Maxx to buy some pants. Previously, their school had sent a letter asking parents not to buy their kids "gangster-looking pants" (the oversized, baggy style that hangs on the hips). Gangster attire had become a popular fad, and the school did not like the image it represented.

When the boys entered the store, they immediately began to beg their mom for the forbidden pants. She reminded them of the school's request and asked them to look for an alternative. Her sons refused to give up. They claimed all their friends were wearing the baggy style and even went so far as to accuse her of wanting them to dress like nerds!

Their mother finally put an end to the dispute.

"One more word about the pants, and you're walking home," she said.

Pretty soon another request came with an added, *Puleeease!*

"That's it!" she said. "I'll see you at the house."

She promptly got in the car and left. An hour later, her sons staggered through the door after trudging a mile and a half uphill. They immediately apologized and asked if they could be taken to the store again—this time with a promise that they wouldn't mention the gangster-looking trousers. Their mother agreed to give them another chance. When they returned to TJ Maxx, the boys selected some other styles, and everyone went home satisfied.

Moral of the story: Learn to be content. If Mom or Dad (or an authority at your school or church) says no to a particular garment or CD, don't argue or demand your own way. Instead, calmly accept their judgment and find an alternative. The apostle Paul said, "I have learned to be content whatever the circumstances" (Philippians 4:11). There's plenty to select from out there, and I'm sure you and your parents can find a happy medium.

Always keep in mind that your mom and dad love you and want the best for you. I'm sure it pleases them to purchase clothes that you like, even if the styles seem a bit strange to them. It hasn't been that long since your parents were in school, and they can remember the desire to dress fashionably.

If money is an issue, you can get a part-time job baby-sitting or mowing lawns. A friend of mine came from a family that couldn't afford to invest in clothes. Instead of complaining, she took a position at a fast-food restaurant to pay for her wardrobe. She was one of the best-dressed girls in school! As the saying goes, "Where there's a will, there's a way."

Your relationship with your parents is too important to fight over trivial matters like clothing and hairstyles. Try to be flexible. This is the best way to help bridge the generation gap. You'll also be pleasing the Lord, who promises to supply your every need.

"Why do you worry about clothes? See how the lilies of the field grow. They do not labor or spin. Yet I tell you that not even Solomon in all his splendor was dressed like one of these. If that is how God clothes the grass of the field, which is here today and to-morrow is thrown into the fire, will he not much more clothe you, O you of little faith?" (Matthew 6:28-30).

your turn

①

Have you and your parents clashed over your taste in such things as clothes, music, or food?

②

If you answered yes to the above question, how have you dealt with these conflicts?

③

How does God want you to respond when you disagree with your mom and dad?

Let's talk about Friends!

She's All That Pajama Party Parameters
A Friendly Shade of Green Fights and Friction
Intolerance

THE BIG LIE

Check It Out!
1 CORINTHIANS 6:19-20

For most people, the junior-high years provide a nonstop series of lessons in life. My experience was no different. Back then, I attended a small Christian school within walking distance of my home. I didn't exactly enjoy having to walk, especially on cold mornings, but after a while I got used to it.

One afternoon, during one of my journeys home, I heard someone call my name. I looked around to see Debbie and Todd, two kids from school, hanging out at a park across the street. I noticed right away that they were smoking cigarettes. Debbie motioned for me to come over.

At first I stood and chatted with them, feeling at ease with the situation. But then the inevitable occurred. Debbie offered me a cigarette. "No thanks," I said. I should have stopped right there, but I felt a need to continue. "It's not like I've never *tried* them before or anything; I just don't feel like it right now."

That was a lie! I had never smoked before, but I wasn't going to risk my status to admit it. Debbie and Todd were part of the "in" crowd at school. I didn't want to leave them with the impression that I was still a child or some kind of "do-gooder." I took the safe route.

When the conversation ended and I turned to leave, the guilt began to set in. I felt foolish and awkward. *Why couldn't I have just said, "No thank you" and let it drop?* I wondered. *Why did I have to tell a big lie?*

Although I sought immediate forgiveness from God, it took a lot longer to confess to Debbie. I finally mustered up the courage at a party years later (using a humorous approach), but by then, Debbie didn't even remember the incident! Well, at least my conscience was cleared.

When I look back on that day at the park, I realize I was completely taken off guard when the cigarette was offered to me. I spoke without having time to think about my words beforehand— I felt backed into a corner. Have you ever been in a similar situation? How did you react? I think it's important to make decisions and rehearse your answers *before* these moments arise. For example, the Bible says, "Have nothing to do with the fruitless deeds of darkness" (Ephesians 5:11). It also says, "He who walks with the wise grows wise, but a companion of fools suffers harm" (Proverbs 13:20). Based on those verses, you can make up your mind now to say no to "fruitless" activities like smoking and to be careful whom you hang out with. Then you won't be tempted to compromise your beliefs or to be dishonest like I was.

Throughout my life, there have been times when others were engaging in activities I chose not to participate in. I never felt disrespected or excluded for standing up for myself. In fact, I was usually admired for choosing to be a nonconformist. One experience that comes to mind is a party that I attended with a friend while we were in college. The party was held at a student's home, so I thought that it would be pretty mellow. I was surprised to see that a number of kids were drinking. Instead of conforming, I chose not to engage in that activity. I sipped a coke and chatted with a few people before leaving. I'll never forget how cool I felt that night! I was doing what I believed was right, and no one pestered me for not drinking alcohol.

People respect those who can say, "No thanks!" and stand by their convictions. It displays confidence! It also sets an example for others who aren't as strong spiritually.

There's a person in the Bible who certainly wasn't afraid to speak his mind—the apostle Paul! In 1 Corinthians 6:19-20, he says: "Do you not know that your body is a temple of the Holy Spirit, who is in you, whom you have received from God? You are not your own; you were bought at a price. Therefore honor God with your body."

We all know that cigarettes are unhealthy, and drugs and alcohol are mind-altering and addictive. By using these substances, we are polluting God's temple; the atmosphere is not a pure and holy place for Him to dwell.

If you're already experimenting with these things, then ask God to help you to stop. If you haven't started, *don't!* Above all, never be afraid to reveal your standards to others. There's nothing like the feeling that comes from showing respect for yourself and honoring God at the same time.

your turn

1
Do you think you're susceptible to peer pressure? What can you do to protect yourself?

2
What will you say to the person who offers you something that is harmful?

3
What is your standard for how to treat your body, God's temple?

INTOLERANCE

Check It Out!
1 PETER 3:15

Not long ago my brother, Ryan, was on a flight to Boise, Idaho. He began chatting with the passenger sitting next to him—a young man named Brandon, who was about the same age. The conversation eventually came to a moral issue that was politically controversial. My brother said he thought the commonly held view was unjust and wrong.

Brandon shrugged. "I don't believe in right or wrong," he said.

He changed the subject and went on to talk about some houseboats that he owned. Apparently, one of the tenants was late in paying rent. Brandon was considering kicking the guy out for his negligence.

My brother immediately recognized a contradiction in the young man's thinking.

"If you don't believe in right or wrong, isn't it okay for the guy not to pay rent?" asked Ryan. "Are you *right* to have him evicted? Is it *wrong* for him to break his contract with you?"

Brandon thought for a moment. "Well," he said, "maybe *subconsciously* I do believe in right and wrong."

When my brother shared that story, I was sad, not only for Brandon, but for millions like him who have been swept up in a wave of relativism. Our nation has entered a new era—one many refer to as *postmodern*. What does that mean? Well, that term refers to a view of the world that denies the existence of God. Postmodern thinkers conclude that there are no rules, nothing is moral or immoral, and anything goes. They say that truth is relative—it's whatever *you* think it is. Postmodernism is not new, however. There was a similar time in the history of ancient Israel when "everyone did as he saw fit" (Judges 21:25). The result was disastrous! When people disregard the God of the universe and His Word, then every form of evil can be rationalized.

As this ideology has spread, the media, schools, and government have increasingly promoted a message of tolerance. You might have heard some of these phrases. They include: "Do your own thing." "Celebrate diversity." "Being gay isn't a choice—choosing a partner is."

The centerpiece of postmodernism is tolerance. It certainly seems to be the buzzword these days, but its definition goes beyond acceptance. As Josh McDowell wrote in his book *The New Tolerance*[3], tolerance preaches that every person's values, opinions, and lifestyle are equally valid. So not only does everyone have a right to his or her own beliefs, but all beliefs are acceptable. The only thing unacceptable is an attitude of intolerance or moral judgment.

I recall a popular song by the artist Jewel that reached the top of the charts. The first line says, "If I could tell the world just one thing, it would be, 'We're all okay.'" Do you understand the message in those lyrics? Jewel is telling us that it doesn't matter what we believe or do. Nothing is required to be a good person—an "okay person"—because nothing is wrong or evil. Of course we should be kind and respectful to everyone, even to those with whom we disagree. But the truth is that some behavior is wicked, and those who commit sins are *not* "okay." They are in need of forgiveness from the only One who can cleanse the soul. This is why we need Jesus as our Savior!

That's what is wrong with this postmodern school of thought. Sadly, our culture has ignored biblical truths and tried to write its

---

[3]Tyndale House Publishers, Inc., 1998.

own script. The result has been a growing acceptance and rationalization of every form of sin.

A recent nationwide study revealed that 10 to 20 percent of college students wouldn't condemn Adolf Hitler. His policies led to the murder of six million Jews, Poles, and political prisoners, not to mention disabled people and preborn babies. He was one of the most wicked tyrants who ever lived, and yet even *he* is not considered "immoral" by one out of five students. One student was quoted as saying, "Of course I dislike the Nazis, but who is to say they are morally wrong?"[4] It's hard to believe we're living in a time when even genocide—the deliberate extermination of a certain group of people—is conceivable.

So what does the Lord require of us in this age of tolerance? We must humbly present the truth! It might be difficult to stand up for what we believe in today's climate, but Ephesians 4:15 commands us to "[speak] the truth in love."

Again, as Josh McDowell has said, we must uphold the truth as a means of *countering* the doctrine of tolerance. It means to embrace all people but not all beliefs. It requires listening to others without necessarily agreeing with them. It means being willing to risk scorn and ridicule for what we believe. 1 Peter 3:15 reminds us, "Always be prepared to give an answer to everyone who asks you to give the reason for the hope that you have. But do this with gentleness and respect."

The Lord may provide opportunities for you to discuss the subject of postmodernism. It might be with a friend or with a stranger (similar to what happened to my brother). You may even find yourself addressing a group on this issue. When it happens, be prepared to point them to the *truth*—the moral absolutes found in the Word of God. There's no celebration of diversity in Scripture—no tolerance of sinful choices or debate over what's right or wrong. But for those who accept and follow the eternal truths, there is meaning, purpose, and peace.

As Jesus told us, "The truth will set [them] free" (John 8:32).

4John Leo, "A No-Fault Holocaust," *U.S. News & World Report,* 21 July 1997.

your turn

❶
Have you witnessed the growing trend toward tolerance and no moral absolutes? In what way(s)?

❷
How can you prepare yourself to avoid being manipulated by these wrong beliefs?

❸
What would you say to a friend who thinks any lifestyle is acceptable and should be tolerated?

"There is a way that seems right to a man,
but in the end it leads to death."

PROVERBS 14:12

SHE'S ALL
THAT!

Check It Out!
JOHN 13:34

So you want to be popular? Who doesn't! Everyone wants to be well liked and accepted. It's essential to know that others want to be in your company.

I attended a public high school where the students were rather cliquish. Sound familiar? Kids there were consumed with fads and fashion and only wanted to associate with those who were popular. To fit in, it was imperative that a person wear the right labels. It wasn't cool to be seen in "knockoff brands"—you had to have the real stuff in order to achieve the look. I admit that I got caught up in this wave, but it was fun to dress trendy.

I noticed something interesting about this scene during those years. Among the attractive students, there were a number of popular kids who didn't score high in the looks department. Especially some of the football players! Their appearance didn't seem to affect their popularity, though. I observed two main characteristics about these teens: First, they all had outgoing, friendly personalities, and second, they were deeply involved in school activities. Whether it was sports or student council, these people were linked in!

What about you? How are you making it through adolescence? The teen years can be wonderful or very difficult, depending largely on how you relate with other students. Let me offer a few ideas that may be helpful at this stage in your life. First, the word "confidence" is the key to all human relationships. Those who reveal it, including the less attractive students, usually get along better with others. Their belief in themselves is like a magnet to which friends are drawn. But if you feel bad about yourself, that attitude will be "read" by other students, and it will push them away. What I'm saying is that it isn't necessary to be a raving beauty or a fashion model to be well liked and respected. If you lack confidence, my advice is to "fake it till you make it." When you start to act self-assured, you will begin to *feel* self-assured, and that will cause your friends to respect you more. But let me make it clear that being self-confident is not the same thing as being arrogant, proud, haughty, or stuck-up. Those are big turnoffs to everyone!

Second, personal grooming is a means of conveying confidence to your associates. Those who don't like themselves often give up on their appearance, going to school with their hair dirty, their teeth scummy, and their clothes rumpled. Even if you can't afford to buy trendy clothes, you can be neat, clean, and well groomed. If you don't care for yourself and your body, no one else will, either.

Third, people are drawn to those who make them feel good about themselves. I remember reading a book in high school called *How to Win Friends and Influence People*. The author emphasized that showing interest in others was a means of building friendships. Skills such as being a good listener, asking questions, and giving compliments are all part of the equation. Of course, I'm not suggesting that you act friendly just so that others will like you. That would be self-serving! But everyone likes to be around someone who's genuinely interested in him or her—don't you?

Fourth, let me say something that may seem contradictory to what I have written so far. While it is fun to be popular and respected, you must not despair if it doesn't happen. You are just getting started in life, and there are important opportunities and experiences to come. When you graduate from high school, that little society you have known will scatter to the four winds. Hopefully you will have made some lasting friendships, but most of the teens you know will go on to many different colleges and other settings. What is happening today won't matter much in the future. Never consider yourself a failure if things go badly in the teen years. The history books are filled with stories of highly successful people who struggled terribly as kids but went on to great accomplishment and fulfillment. God is not through with you yet!

Fifth and finally, the most important thing is to find your place in the kingdom of Jesus Christ. He knows where you are and has a job for you to do. Young people who understand this mission have a better grip on "the meaning of life" and an awareness that they are never alone.

I know a guy who started a Friday-night Bible study at church. He would regularly play his guitar with a worship team and then share a thought about our Christian faith. Before long, his Bible study grew to more than one hundred attendees! When it came time for this young man's birthday, a huge surprise party was planned. There were skits, songs, and a festive cake to commemorate the occasion. Many people shared how their lives had been touched through his ministry. The evening finally ended with one hundred people singing "Happy Birthday."

This guy didn't set out to become "Mr. Popular"—he only wanted to serve the Lord. But in doing so, he received the blessing of being respected and well liked by his peers.

I realize that it doesn't always work this way. Some of us are criticized or even persecuted for our beliefs. Jesus told us to expect that. But you can't go wrong in investing in people's lives. That's what Christianity is all about. Perhaps Jesus said it best when He gave this commandment: "Love one another. As I have loved you, so you must love one another. By this all men will know that you are my disciples, if you love one another" (John 13:34-35).

Whether you're witnessing for Christ, joining forces in prayer, or helping someone in need, you're exercising Jesus' commandment. Not only is this the right thing to do, but it's also a great avenue to meaningful friendships!

your turn

①

Do you feel accepted by your peers?

②

Would you like to have more friends? If so, think of some ways that you can be a friend to others.

③

Name a Christian peer whom you admire. Jot down three characteristics about that person that appeal to you, and try to imitate those characteristics this week.

④

Think of two friends who are going through a difficult time. Why not give them an "encouragement phone call" this week?

HE SAID/ SHE SAID

Check It Out!
EPHESIANS 4:29-32

Brenda: Did you hear that David and Jessica broke up?

Rachel: No way! Really?

Brenda: Yeah! I heard that they got into a fight because Jessica was flirting with Kevin.

Rachel: Kevin McCormick? He's such a geek!

Brenda: *Major* geek! I don't know *why* Jessica would risk her relationship with David for someone like Kevin.

Rachel: Totally! So why did they break up?

Brenda: Well, I heard that David told Jessica that she'd better start acting like his girlfriend instead of a free agent.

Rachel: He did? What did Jessica say to *that*?

Brenda: She accused David of being a big control freak and told him to grow up.

Rachel: Then what happened?

Brenda: They argued until David finally told her that he wanted to break up with her. Jessica's been taking it pretty hard since he slammed the phone down in her ear. Rumor has it that she's been trying to get back together with him. I don't think it's gonna happen, though. David won't take her calls.

Rachel: Wow! Who'd you hear all this stuff from?

Brenda: Lisa Samuels—she talked to David's best friend and got the scoop from him.
Rachel: Wait till I tell my sister; she's had a crush on David all year!

Does this conversation sound familiar? If you haven't done the "dishing," you've probably been the victim of it. Let's face it—gossiping about people can be a lot of fun!

Why do we enjoy talking about others behind their backs? Probably the most obvious reason is because it makes us feel better about ourselves. When we discuss someone's personal life, especially if there's baggage, we are trying to build ourselves up. It's also more interesting to divulge juicy information than common knowledge. Someone once said, "Gossipers are like vultures—they like their meat rancid." Consider the popularity of tabloid newspapers such as the *National Enquirer* and *Star*. The covers usually picture a celebrity who is in some kind of mess. People must love to read these scandalous stories, because tabloids sell millions of copies each week! Just the other day I saw this headline while standing in line at the supermarket: "Top Five Messiest Celebrity Divorces." Their readers are obviously intrigued by a little dirt and a good scandal. I even heard a tabloid editor confess one time that positive cover stories don't sell magazines.

In 1990 I wrote a children's book called *Woof and the Haunted House*. Perhaps you read it when you were younger. The message centered around gossiping and the importance of telling the truth. In the story, two children and their dog, Woof, explore an old house that is rumored to be haunted. A wild tale had spread throughout the town about the elderly man who used to live there. He had been dead for years, but folks were certain he was still lurking around the rickety house. Some claimed to have heard strange noises there, while others insisted that they'd actually seen the old man on the property! These stories fascinate Mark and Krissy—so much that they decide to take Woof in to investigate. Of course, they end up discovering that the rumors aren't true, but not before a loud crash convinces them otherwise. Eventually, Woof discovers a stray cat in the closet—mystery solved!

The Scripture I chose for this story was James 3:5 (NLT): "The tongue is a small thing, but what enormous damage it can do." In real life, gossip focuses not on a haunted house, but on people who get badly hurt by those who talk behind their backs.

When I was in the seventh grade, one of the girls in my class was absent for a month while she recovered from an illness. During that time a vicious rumor started going around that she had suffered a heart attack. You can imagine how she felt when she finally returned to school. Fellow classmates were constantly approaching her and asking, "Are you okay? We heard you had a heart attack!" The poor girl was horrified and went home in tears that day. I can remember our homeroom teacher chastising the class. She couldn't believe anyone would start such a malicious rumor! We never did find out who the culprit was, but I had my suspicions.

Is it any wonder that the Bible compares the power of the tongue to a raging fire? In James 3.6 we're told that the tongue has the capacity to corrupt a person and alter the entire course of his or her life. Pretty intense for such a small part of the body!

When we use our tongue to spread gossip or to criticize someone, we reveal what's inside our own hearts, which is often jealousy and bitterness. We also send a message that we can't be trusted. No one wants to confide in someone who's been labeled a "big talker." You can't build emotional intimacy with a person like that. Imagine a friend just finished telling you the latest about someone you knew. Would you then feel safe revealing anything personal to that friend? I wouldn't! In fact, I'd be extremely guarded. If the gossiper would trash someone else in front of you, he or she would probably slam *you* when your back was turned.

Hey, the majority of us love to talk about everything under the sun. But we're not always aware of the damage of those casual words. A good Bible passage to remember is Ephesians 4:29-30: "Do not let any unwholesome talk come out of your mouths, but only what is helpful for building others up according to their needs, that it may benefit those who listen. And do not grieve the Holy Spirit of God, with whom you were sealed for the day of redemption."

Remember this verse the next time you're conversing with someone. Ask yourself, *Are my words kind? Are they uplifting? Would I mind if the person I'm talking about was listening?* Likewise, as soon as a friend starts gossiping, call her attention to it in a polite way or simply change the subject. In doing so, you'll be promoting trustworthiness among your circle of friends. Those relationships will be free to deepen and grow without the hindrance of negativity. You'll also be pleasing the Lord by keeping "slander" and "bitterness" out of your conversations. Who wants to dwell on garbage anyway? Isn't it more fun to concentrate on topics of substance . . . like, uh, cute guys, for instance?

your turn

1

Be honest with yourself. Do you spread gossip or bad-mouth people when they're not around? Would your friends agree with your answer?

2

What will you do the next time you're tempted to gossip about or criticize someone?

3

How will you handle it when a friend starts to gossip?

"May the God who gives endurance and encouragement give you a spirit of unity among yourselves as you follow Christ Jesus, so that with one heart and mouth you may glorify the God and Father of our Lord Jesus Christ."

ROMANS 15:5-6

CAT FIGHTS AND FRICTION

Check It Out!
EPHESIANS 4:31-32

Jennifer and Lorrie were "thick as thieves," as the saying goes. They spent all of their spare time together—shopping, going to movies, or just hanging out. When they weren't in one another's company, they were on the telephone, giggling and talking about the fun things in their lives. The two girls were best friends, in the truest sense. In fact, they each had half of a "Best Friends" gold heart charm, which they sometimes wore to school. The necklaces symbolized how close they were.

Unfortunately, their relationship took a nasty turn during their junior year. That's when Lorrie began dating Trey, a guy she met at church. Suddenly Lorrie didn't have as much time for Jennifer and, quite frankly, she preferred to spend every waking moment with her boyfriend. To make matters worse, Trey and Jennifer didn't hit it off very well. They each were jealous of the role the other played in Lorrie's life.

Jennifer gradually felt abandoned by her best friend. The more time that elapsed, the more bitter and envious she became. But instead of sitting down with Lorrie to discuss her feelings, Jennifer switched into attack mode. She began harassing Lorrie about her boyfriend. One of her frequent complaints was, "Trey is more important to you than I am!" She also looked for opportunities to criticize Trey. Once while she and Lorrie were alone, Jennifer pointed out that she thought he was immature. She even went so far as to say that he wasn't good enough for Lorrie. It was a case of green-eyed envy, pure and simple.

That was the final straw! Lorrie left Jennifer in the lurch and refused to talk to her. Her parting words were, "If you can't accept my boyfriend, then I can't accept you!"

How could two friends who used to be so close end up angry and resentful toward one another? If you think this situation is rare, guess again. It happens way too often! You may have already experienced it to one degree or another with your own friends. I know that I have!

Of course, this is only one scenario. Conflicts between close friends can deteriorate into competitiveness, cruel words, disagreements, back-stabbing antics, or miscommunication. Sometimes one person will lose interest in the friendship and stop making an effort. This, too, can cause hurt feelings and resentment for the other. Basically, whenever two people form an emotional bond, there is potential for conflict.

Disagreements are inevitable, but what counts is how you deal with them. This is where spiritual wisdom comes into play. The mature Christian uses good judgment when working toward conflict resolution. For the sake of comparison, I've written some possible right and wrong ways to settle a feud.

Immature Reactions to Conflict

- Arguing
- Shouting or raising your voice
- Giving the silent treatment
- Bad-mouthing your adversary to others behind his or her back
- Saying or doing things to hurt the person
- Ending the friendship altogether

Mature Reactions to Conflict

- Getting together with the person and rationally discussing your feelings

- "Biting your tongue" when you want to say something harsh
- Keeping a calm tone of voice
- Resolving the matter ASAP
- Offering a spirit of forgiveness
- Asking the Lord to help you and your friend to overcome differences

Which category are *you* more apt to follow?

Although my list is not taken directly from Scripture, it does coincide with biblical instruction. Check out Ephesians 4:31-32: "Get rid of all bitterness, rage and anger, brawling and slander, along with every form of malice. Be kind and compassionate to one another, forgiving each other, just as in Christ God forgave you."

The apostle Paul told us very clearly, "In your anger do not sin" (Ephesians 4:26). He was acknowledging that we are emotional creatures who cannot help feeling irritated or hurt; it's what we do with those feelings that can become sinful. In other words, one can't help what he or she feels, which is involuntary. We *are* accountable, however, for how we react to those feelings. Attempting to hurt or embarrass or belittle the one who has wounded you is wrong.

Resentment can also become like a cancer on the soul. As my pastor once said during a sermon: "If there's a root of bitterness beginning to dig down deep and then spring up—stop everything you're doing—everything. Go to the root of it, find out the reason, gain forgiveness for yourself, give forgiveness to everyone else, and be cleansed from it. Don't let anything deter you." This message is proclaimed throughout the New Testament.

When I was a little girl, my mother frequently quoted Ephesians 4:26: "Do not let the sun go down while you are still angry." There's a good reason for this command: The longer you remain angry, the more bitterness will creep into your life. It will affect your personality, making you a negative and unhappy person. Bitterness will hurt you more than it will hurt the one who wounded you. That is why the sooner you admit that you're angry and confess it to God, the better.

It is inevitable that people are going to tick you off—that's life. But God can change your feelings and attitudes through the gift of His grace. He can give you the ability to forgive your offender and to put the matter to rest. Trust Him on this!

As for Jennifer and Lorrie, I'm happy to report that they've resumed their friendship, even though Lorrie still has a boyfriend and Jennifer does not. The two girls finally discovered that a little love and forgiveness can go a long way toward mending broken "Best Friends" hearts.

your turn

❶

According to the Bible, when is it wrong to be angry with someone? (See Proverbs 14:17, Ecclesiastes 7:9, and Matthew 5:22.)

❷

In what ways can your anger become displeasing to the Lord?

❸

Is there an unresolved conflict between you and another person? If so, what can you do to restore the friendship?

AN UGLY SHADE OF GREEN

Check It Out!
James 3:14,16

Do any of these remarks sound familiar?
- "Here comes Mark with his prissy little girlfriend! What does he see in her?"
- "The only reason Samantha has nice clothes is that her mother buys them for her."
- "Kelly thinks she's so cool because she's a cheerleader."
- "I can't stand to be around Jennifer—I'm sick of hearing about her perfect life!"

You've probably heard criticisms similar to these. Maybe you've also been guilty of resenting others. We all have a tendency to feel jealous from time to time—people can be very competitive. We compare what we have to another girl's beauty or boyfriend or material possessions. We become angry when a sibling gets something we wanted. The inability to achieve the same fortune makes us "green with envy." As a result, we might be tempted to say or do things to deceive or hurt the other person.

A good example of jealousy and where it can lead is the story of Cain and Abel (Genesis 4). As you may recall, the two brothers presented different sacrifices before the Lord. Cain, a farmer, gave some "fruits of the soil" (meaning grain), but Abel offered the firstborn of his flock of sheep. The Lord was pleased with Abel's gift, but He didn't approve of Cain's offering. Cain became very angry. His hatred burned so greatly that he attacked his brother and killed him!

Most people would never go that far, but this story reminds us of how jealousy can take over our emotions. It's important to keep a handle on jealousy in our relationships.

In Matthew 22:39 Jesus says, "Love your neighbor as yourself." Let's concentrate on the true meaning of this command. What does it mean to love? "Love is patient, love is kind. It does not envy, it does not boast, it is not proud. It is not rude, it is not self-seeking, it is not easily angered, it keeps no record of wrongs" (1 Corinthians 13:4-5).

It's impossible to love our neighbor while struggling with jealousy at the same time. It's also not very "Christlike"!

Over the years, there have been times when I've felt envious toward someone, and there have been friends who have felt that way toward me. One girl even admitted she was jealous of me during a heart-to-heart discussion! Although it's natural to have these emotions, jealousy is harmful to our spiritual and emotional well-being. It needs to be dealt with and eliminated ASAP. Here's how to get rid of the green-eyed monster in three steps.

❶ Pray that God would help you overcome your weakness in this area. "I can do all things through Christ who strengthens me" (Philippians 4:13, NKJV).

❷ Stop comparing yourself to other people. There is always going to be someone who is prettier or richer or more popular. Remember that love "does not envy." A loving attitude is one of acceptance and joy for another person's success. This is a reflection of spiritual maturity. "Let us not become conceited, provoking and envying each other" (Galatians 5:26).

❸ Focus on your own blessings! There is so much to thank God for—even things that we sometimes take for granted, like eyesight and a healthy mind. Whenever I start to consider what I don't have, I remember to thank God for what I've already been given. The list just keeps adding up!

Not long ago, a friend gave me a small novelty box that says "Count Your Blessings." All I have to do is look at that box to be inspired. "O Lord my God, I will give you thanks forever" (Psalm 30:12).

Try this: Make a list of all the gifts that God has given you; then praise Him for His goodness. When you do this, the smaller things in life—such as the fact that your best friend has a boyfriend and you don't—will seem relatively insignificant. Your heart will become so full of thanksgiving that it will be difficult to complain about anything.

The next time you're tempted to turn into the "green-eyed monster," stop and talk to God about it. Ask Him to help you deal with your feelings of jealousy. Then, take a moment to concentrate on your list of the many gifts God has given you. As you keep adding more blessings to it, I think you'll find that life really isn't that unfair!

your turn

❶
Are you jealous of anyone? What is causing you to feel this way?

❷
In what ways has jealousy affected your behavior?

❸
The next time you feel envious of someone, how will you work on overcoming it?

PJ PARTY PARAMETERS

Check It Out!
1 CORINTHIANS 10:31-32

Do you enjoy a good slumber party? Is staying up half the night talking or watching videos your idea of fun?

I've always loved this sort of thing! When I was in junior high, my parents let me invite the girls in my class to spend the night. It was a memorable experience—twelve adolescent females under one roof! We spent the evening chomping on pizza, talking about cute boys, and giggling in our sleeping bags until we finally crashed at 2:00 A.M. That night remains one of the highlights of my younger years—I remember it as though it were yesterday.

Recently, I had lunch with a girlfriend who attended that slumber party. During our conversation, she brought up the event and recalled how much fun it was. She remembered the classmates who were there and the games we played. It made me feel good to know that she had special memories from my party.

I also loved my pop-up tent, which I set up in the backyard. I used to invite a girlfriend over, and we'd talk for hours (until we had to come into the house at midnight). When I got a little older, my brother, Ryan, took possession of the tent. Sometimes I would look out the window and see the glow of his flashlight through the vinyl doorway. Ryan and his friend, Craig, loved to "camp" in the backyard. There was something about it that fueled their imaginations.

Whether you're "camping" or just hanging out, it's great to be with friends when the sun goes down. Pj's, chocolate-chip cookies, and spooky stories can add to the amusement.

One of my favorite teen memories was an "antislumber party" (no sleep!) that was held at my Sunday-school teacher's home. She made a bowl of homemade caramel corn, and a group of us stayed up all night watching movies. The VCR was still going at ten o'clock the next morning! It wasn't the most original idea, but for a girl who was used to bedtimes and curfews, I thought it was great.

In light of what I've been describing, how sad I am to hear that slumber parties are beginning to lose their innocence. Focus on the Family, a ministry in Colorado, often receives letters from girls who are concerned about one of the current fads—dabbling in the occult. This growing fascination with séances, Ouija boards, tarot cards, levitation, and the Wicca religion is not something to mess with! The Bible is unyielding about the importance of staying out of the satanic world. Check out what the apostle Paul has to say in 1 Corinthians 10: "I do not want you to be participants with demons. You cannot drink the cup of the Lord and the cup of demons too; you cannot have a part in both the Lord's table and the table of demons" (vv. 20-21). If you're at a party that starts to head in this direction, *leave!* You'd be better off finding a group of friends who want to engage in a Bible study.

Another distressing activity involves bunking with the opposite sex. Evidently, coed sleepovers are becoming as common as pep rallies!

Michelle Malkin described this trend in an article she wrote for Creators Syndicate, Inc. These are her words: "All across the country, believe it or not, adolescent boys and girls are romping around in their skivvies together under one roof with their parents' approval. The *Washington Post* devoted 1,200 words to this booming teen fad. A newspaper database search turned up nearly two hundred other stories on coed sleepovers. Popular teen TV shows such as the WB network's *7th Heaven* have featured boy-girl slumber parties. An Abercrombie & Fitch Christmas catalog featured four preteen girls in bed under the covers with an older boy, lewdly waving his boxer shorts in the air. 'It's the newest thing,' one seventeen-year-old boy named J. D. explained to the *Post* reporter. Some parents say the parties became more common a couple of years ago after school administrators in several districts asked hotels to stop providing rooms to students after big high-school events. To win over his parents, J. D. argued that hosting a coed slumber party is 'better than us lying about where we are and renting some sleazy motel room.'"[5]

Does this sound right to you? It seems that J. D. is a master of manipulation.

I came across a better argument in the same passage we read earlier. 1 Corinthians 10:31-32 says, "Whether you eat or drink or whatever you do, do it all for the glory of God. Do not cause anyone to stumble."

Obviously, a bunch of guys and girls running around in nightwear are going to cause one another to stumble, if only in their minds. It doesn't take much to "stoke the fire," and coed sleepovers are asking for trouble.

God created us as sexual beings; He made us vulnerable this way. It's natural to have desires, but the danger lies in giving in to those feelings before marriage. Many times sex occurs between two people who didn't really plan to do it; the forces were set in motion and took over from there.

You might be thinking to yourself, "I'm strong enough to avoid that temptation," and you may be right; but why take a chance? And what about the guy on the sofa next to you? Will he have the same self-control?

Here's a solution: The next time you have a slumber party, why not engage in some good, clean fun? Start by inviting your girlfriends over for a little pampering—facials and manicures—and do something creative together, like rearranging your bedroom, making yummy desserts, or working on a fun project. Then

---

[5]Michelle Malkin, "Baby Boomer Parents Are Asleep on the Job," Creators Syndicate, 17 November 2000. By permission of Michelle Malkin and Creators Syndicate, Inc.

eat some munchies, watch a cool (and decent!) flick, and talk about guys until you drop off to sleep. I guarantee that it will be an evening well spent, sans the mischief.

your turn

1

When you go to a slumber party, what activities do you like to participate in?

2

If you were invited to a coed sleepover, what would you do?

3

As a Christian, how can you be an example regarding slumber parties?

LIGHT THE WAY

Check It Out!
MATTHEW 5:16

September 11, 2001—commonly referred to as "the worst day in American history." Terrorist attacks—smoke—flames—collapsing towers. None of us will ever forget the images that we saw when the World Trade Center and the Pentagon were attacked. It was devastating!

Shortly thereafter I received a card from a friend. The photo on the front displayed a cross of steel beams. You may have seen the same picture in a newspaper, magazine, or on television. A laborer found the image standing amidst the rubble in New York two days after the tragedy. It was truly a remarkable metaphor for what had just occurred. One Christian commentator referred to it as "a symbol of victory over evil and death." He reminded us that what man intends for evil, God often uses for good.

Just think of the changes that have occurred since September 11, 2001. The phrase "In God We Trust" has appeared on billboards, bumper stickers, and television programs throughout the country. People have been asking the right questions and are more receptive to hearing the gospel. For Christians, this represents an opportunity to have enormous impact! For the first time in many years, a barrier has been broken. In a way it reminds me of the demolition of the Berlin Wall that occurred in 1989. It was a red-letter day in world history. The Soviet Union had built the barrier to keep East Germans from fleeing from their oppressive region after World War II. On one side (the West) was freedom, and on the other (the East) was tyranny and dictatorship. Those who tried to escape were shot! Then suddenly, everything changed. The Soviet Union unraveled, and the Wall came down. The old rules and restrictions disappeared, and freedom reigned for the first time in nearly forty-five years.

Since the tragedy of September 11, another "wall" seems to be crumbling. Whereas it has been "politically incorrect" to mention God or Jesus Christ, or even to admit that evil exists, I sense a new freedom in this country. Many people have begun searching for truth and faith.

I don't mean to imply that moral relativism is a thing of the past. On the contrary. Just this week I heard a song on the radio with these lyrics:

> We all live under the same sky
> We all will live, we all will die
> There is no wrong, there is no right
> The circle only has one side.[6]

The ideology of "no absolute truth" is still alive and flourishing within our schools. But even with the popularity of this unfortunate worldview, some people are inquiring about the meaning of life. They want to know why they're here, what their purpose is, and how God fits into the plan. As Christians, we have the answers to their questions! The time is right for us to step up to the plate and boldly make our witness known.

For me personally, this means using my writing and speaking as a form of ministry. Last December my mother and I spoke to a large crowd of women at a Christmas luncheon. We talked candidly about our family traditions, such as prayer, and discussed the importance of having faith in Christ. By the time we finished, some of the ladies had made a decision to receive Jesus as their Savior! One of them worked for the catering company that provided the food that afternoon. It was really exciting to see God at work!

---

[6]"Side" © 2001 by Travis. Published by Sony. From the CD *The Invisible Band* © 2001 Sony/ATV Music Publishing.

I share this story not to sound self-righteous, but to emphasize the fact that people are searching for answers and they're hungry for the gospel.

Will you do *your* part in spreading the good news? The opportunities are all around you, but they may not last. Here are some ways that you can make an impact for Christ right now:

- Share your faith with a non-Christian friend. (Suggestion: Use your own testimony of how God saved you and what He is doing in your life.)
- Confront someone who is practicing a false "religion," such as New Age. This is difficult, so be sure to prepare ahead of time: pray, read the Bible so you'll know the truth, seek advice, and rehearse what you plan to say to your friend. When the time comes to share, remember to "[speak] the truth in love" (Ephesians 4:15).
- Volunteer for a local ministry that is trying to have an influence for Christ. Support them financially.
- Reach out to someone who is hurting, sick, poor, or depressed.
- Go on a missions trip with your church or another ministry. (There are usually "work and witness" teams in the summer months. You can help your church during the school year, too, by getting involved in community projects.)
- Pray and ask the Lord to direct you to the area of greatest need.

When my brother graduated from college, my dad spoke at the commencement ceremony. I'll always remember what he said at the conclusion of his message:

When you come to the end of your life, and you look back on the things that you're the most proud of, you're not going to care about the honors you achieved, the businesses you owned, and the money you made. Those things will be relatively unimportant to you. What will matter the most are the people whom you loved, those who loved you, and what you did together in service for the Lord. Everything else will pale in comparison. If you're going to feel that way then . . . why not live that way now?

At the time, my dad's words made a lot of sense to me. In light of the tragedies that occurred in New York and Washington, D.C., I agree with him even more today. All that matters in life are our relationships and what we do in service for the Lord. These are the only things that we can take with us to heaven for eternity. When I consider this fact, the need to reach others for Christ becomes all the more significant. Each one of us should be doing our part to be of service to the Lord.

In Matthew 9:36-38, we are told that Jesus had compassion on the crowds that had gathered in front of Him. He saw that they were "harassed and helpless, like sheep without a shepherd." He told His disciples, "The harvest is plentiful but the workers are few. Ask the Lord of the harvest, therefore, to send out workers into his harvest field."

Are you prepared to be one of God's workers? The job requirements are as follows: dedication, diligence, an understanding of biblical truth, a foundation of faith, and a love for people.

Will you roll up your sleeves and enter the harvest field? God has a special assignment just for you.

your turn

①

How would you respond if a friend turned to you and asked, "Why are you a Christian?"

②

Write down the name of someone who is an unbeliever. Think of one way that you can be a "light" to that person. Pray for him or her.

③

As a Christian, you have been given spiritual gifts and talents. Seek the Lord's direction in using those assets in the world around you. Why not take a moment right now to ask Him what you can do in His service? Jot down any thoughts that come to your mind.

*"Let your light shine before men,
that they may see your good deeds
and praise your Father in heaven."*

MATTHEW 5:16

Let's talk about GUYS!

HE'S SOOO FINE

Check It Out!
PROVERBS 3:21-23

When you have a crush on a guy, are you guilty of any of the following?

- Staring at him when he's not looking
- Conveniently planting yourself near his locker
- Dialing his phone number and hanging up
- Showing off or flirting to capture his attention
- Getting your friends to find out juicy bits of information about him

If you answered yes to any of the above, then I encourage you to read on!

It's amazing the lengths to which a girl will go when she is obsessed with someone. I happen to be an expert on this subject, because I've done a few crazy stunts myself.

During my junior year of high school, there was a guy who sat next to me in English. He flirted with me a few times, and by midsemester I was hooked. I began trying to capture his interest in a myriad of ways, including flirting and writing him clever little notes in class. I even persuaded my girlfriend to approach him on the PE field and tell him I liked him. Big mistake! She returned with the heartbreaking news that I had confused his signals. . . . He had his eye on someone else!

Having survived a few scrapes like that has taught me some valuable lessons. The most important among them is the observation that no matter how much you like someone, your self-respect comes first. I realize it's easy to lose sight of this when you're crazy about a guy, but you need to keep a tight rein on your feelings. You can't make someone desire you no matter how hard you try. There's a place for subtle flirting and making yourself available to someone you like. That's the way "the game" is played, and it's a fun thing to do. But it must stay within certain limits. It's a turnoff to be too aggressive and silly with a guy. The best way to draw someone to you is to show that you have confidence in yourself and are fun to be with. Anything beyond that merely makes you look foolish.

Over the years, I've developed my own set of guidelines that are safe to practice around the opposite sex. If you're like me, when you're attracted to someone, you want to take an immediate course of action. The following tips may be helpful to you when you're madly "in like":

- Take the time to look your personal best. You want him to notice you, right?
- Don't be a loud, knee-slapping comedian. Guys like to joke around with funny girls, but goofy behavior can squelch romantic interest.
- If he teases and flirts with you, it's okay to reciprocate . . . just don't overdo it.
- Be careful about what information you share with your friends. Someone once said, "Either a secret is too good to keep or not good enough." People love to talk! Everything shared in secret will eventually be revealed.
- Don't "just happen" to be in places where he hangs out. If he's interested in you, he knows where to find you.
- Watch your verbal and nonverbal cues. It's good for him to wonder about your feelings—a little mystery is healthy.
- Do not make out and get physical with a guy to try to capture or hold him. And by all means, *do not* sleep with anyone! You will end up feeling used and alone.

Premarital sex is also contradictory to God's law, which was created for our good.

• Ask the Lord for wisdom and direction!

In this and every other aspect of life, I urge you to stay close to God and look to Him to meet your needs. He made you and understands how your emotions function. He has a definite plan for your life, and you must not get ahead of Him.

Life has enough pain without adding grief from the opposite sex. When we try to make things happen on our own, we risk getting hurt. Our advances may be met with rejection or cutting remarks. There's a verse in Proverbs that says, "My son, preserve sound judgment and discernment, do not let them out of your sight; they will be life for you, an ornament to grace your neck. Then you will go on your way in safety, and your foot will not stumble" (3:21-23).

One of the best ways to exercise judgment is through prayer. The Lord cares about every aspect of our lives. He created the concept of love and marriage, so He understands our fascination with guys. When we commit our desires to Him, we have the assurance that His perfect plan will be revealed.

So if it's His will for you to end up with your "heartthrob," then nothing will get in the way. But don't be discouraged if it doesn't happen—the Lord has someone much better for you!

your turn

❶
Have you made mistakes with guys you were attracted to? What did you learn in the process?

❷
What's one guideline you can follow next time you're around a guy you like?

❸
Name three ways you can rely on the Lord for direction.

IT'S A DATE

Check It Out!
GALATIANS 5:22

Suppose you're attracted to a guy at church. He's funny, intelligent, and totally gorgeous. You smile and flirt a little when you're around him, just to let him know you're interested. He reciprocates, and before long your wish has come true—HE ASKS YOU OUT ON A DATE! (Don't you wish it were always this easy?)

So now you're contemplating the big night. What will you wear? How will the conversation go? Can you keep from tripping over the curb or spilling iced tea down your dress?

There are few things in life more nerve-racking than a first date, especially with someone you're crazy about. But what makes you decide whether or not to go out with that person in the first place?

Some of you may think dating is a bad idea, and there's certainly a valid argument for that point of view (see "Waiting for Dating?" on page 123). But whether you are already hitting the scene or just wondering what to look for in a future husband, it would be a good idea to think through some of the basics.

First, keep in mind that you should not even consider going out with non-Christian guys. Period! There's too much at stake to take a chance on an unbeliever, so I recommend that you not "go there." Of course, this doesn't imply that Christian guys are perfect, but at least you're protecting yourself from ending up with someone who doesn't share your values. That concept is in agreement with 2 Corinthians 6:14: "Do not be yoked together with unbelievers."

Once you've committed to date only Christian guys (I hope), you need to identify the qualities in a future husband that are important to you. Someone suggested making a list and dividing it into categories. I've done this, and it proved useful in helping me understand what I cared about. Some of the categories I emphasized were spiritual and moral characteristics, personality traits, physical attributes, and overall interests. A sense of humor and an ability to have fun are also important to me. In each section, I wrote specific qualities to define what I wanted. I also made a list of what I was *not* interested in. I thought it was a good idea to put these negative points on paper, so my better judgment wouldn't be clouded by infatuation.

Some flaws are obvious, though. For instance, there's a guy in one of my classes who's handsome and well dressed, but his arrogant personality is a turnoff! He has to be the expert on everything, no matter what we're discussing. Bummer, because I'd probably be interested in him if he weren't such a know-it-all. The Bible warns against pride. Consider Proverbs 8:13: "To fear the Lord is to hate evil; I hate pride and arrogance." So, for me, arrogance is a deal breaker, no matter how attractive a guy is. What are some traits that turn *you* off?

Sometimes a red flag will pop up when you first meet someone. I'm reminded of what Jesus said in Matthew 7:20: "By their fruit you will recognize them." I often think of this verse when it comes to the opposite sex. I can usually get a hint of where a guy is spiritually in the first five minutes of conversation. Can you? If you're uncertain, just watch for the clues. If he brags on himself, talks about money too much, or mentions a wild party he just attended, then move on. There could be a rotten piece of fruit on that tree!

In Galatians 5:22-23 we're told that "the fruit of the Spirit is love, joy, peace, patience, kindness, goodness, faithfulness, gentleness and self-control." Anybody who is walking with the Lord should mirror these qualities. You can't be filled with God's Spirit without revealing it to others. That's why Jesus said we would recognize a true believer by his fruit. By that, He was referring to the good that comes from a person's heart. "Every good tree bears good fruit, but a bad tree bears bad fruit" (Matthew 7:17).

Now that we've covered the basics, let's focus on the actual date. Here's my suggestion: If a guy asks you out and you want to go, why not make it a "group thing"? If you and your date hang out with friends, it will be less stressful and perhaps a lot more fun. Not only that, but it will keep your relationship from getting serious. The last thing you need during your teen years is to get tied down—you have the rest of your life for that! Adolescence is a time to be free and enjoy many friends, both guys and girls.

I had a boyfriend whom I really liked when I was a junior in high school. We liked to hang out together, but we spent most of our time with friends from church. We played volleyball, racquetball, and joined in on ski trips and parties. We had a blast! When I look back on those days, I remember them as one of the highlights of my life. The youth group at church was so much fun to interact with! I don't think my boyfriend and I could have had a better time by ourselves.

There's another reason why it's good to congregate in groups—it lessens the possibility of sexual temptation. When you're alone with a guy, the setting is a lot more intimate. This can provoke emotions leading to physical familiarity. By mixing with groups, you can avoid the temptation to compromise your standards and the things that God has reserved for married couples.

Of course, there may be exceptions to the "group policy." Sometimes a guy will ask you to accompany him to a specific function alone, such as a concert or a baseball game. I think it's okay to accept an invitation like this, as long as you feel comfortable with him (and your parents approve). There's no sense in creating a list of hard-and-fast rules that can't be altered. Just be careful to "guard your heart" (Proverbs 4:23). There is an interesting thing about girls. . . . They tend to be more emotional than guys and as a result are the ones who often get hurt the most when a relationship dies.

I often think of a line my dad used to say to me: "Keep it light and easy!" That's good advice to follow in regard to friendships with guys. A light and easy approach doesn't move too fast or place heavy demands on anyone. It doesn't have high expectations, and it isn't sexually familiar. This minimizes the fighting and arguing. The result is fun and laughter without pain and aggravation. If you'll remember the "light and easy" rule, it will help you in your relationships.

Let me leave you with a final thought: One of God's greatest gifts is the attraction between males and females. When the chemistry is right, it can be a bigger thrill than a seven-loop roller coaster! But just like all of God's ideas, there are certain principles you must adhere to. I often hear girls say things such as, "I went out with the nicest guy last weekend—he's not a believer, but he went to a Christian school for six years." Or, "Yes, I know that he parties a lot, but I'm hoping that I can have a positive influence on him." Lotsa luck!

Don't be like the girls who rationalize. Check your motives! Are you interested in following the Lord or doing your own thing? Read the Bible and ask God for wisdom and guidance. He longs to help you develop healthy friendships with guys, minus the scrapes!

your turn

①
What did Jesus mean when He said, "By their fruit you will recognize them"?

②
How can you apply that to your interactions with the opposite sex?

③
In regard to dating, what should be your number-one priority?

④
What are some characteristics in a guy that are important to you? (Why not take a sheet of paper and make a list? Keep it handy for review.)

⑤
Think of two reasons why "group dating" is a good idea.

THANKS, BUT NO THANKS

Check It Out!
2 Corinthians 6:14

"So many men, so little time!"

Have you heard or seen that slogan around town? It's usually on bumper stickers and license-plate frames. The message implies that there's an abundance of available guys and that women should be chalking up as many conquests as possible. It sounds innocent enough. . . . After all, what could be more fun than fluttering from one romantic encounter to another?

However, that attitude has its downside. What began as a casual encounter can lead to something more serious than you intended. Also, some of the "available guys" might have values that are totally different from your own. That's why we Christians should follow some scriptural principles in choosing whom to date. Specifically, as I mentioned in a previous chapter, we should associate only with Christian guys, and even then, discretion is required. Not everyone who claims to be a believer really "walks the talk," and those who do still have flaws that can clash with your own. When it comes to dating, a good rule of thumb is to "proceed with caution."

You may have heard stories of Christians marrying unbelievers and leading them to the Lord. Sure, it happens occasionally, but it's risky business. There's no guarantee, and a lot of things can go haywire along the way.

Do you remember how God banned the Israelites from inter-marrying in ancient times? In Deuteronomy 7, He prohibited them from pairing up with people from other nations. This was because He knew the Israelites would be tempted to worship for-eign idols and other false gods.

My friend Jennifer is an example of why it is unwise to fall in love with someone who doesn't share your faith. She lived the life of a solid Christian for most of her twenty-four years . . . until she met Rick. He was a nice guy with a charming personality, but his religious background was completely different from Jennifer's. Like other people who fall hard for someone, Jennifer believed she could win her partner to the Lord. She felt safe in accepting Rick's marriage proposal.

Less than two years into the marriage, the tables turned. In-stead of Rick becoming a Christian, Jennifer adopted his value system. Friends and family members warned her that it was a mis-take, but their words only made her resentful. Jennifer wanted to be in agreement with her husband, so she compromised and al-tered her religious beliefs.

Today, she is still practicing a false religion that contradicts the Bible. To make matters worse, she and Rick now have chil-dren who are being exposed to these lies. This was a conse-quence of Jennifer choosing to get involved with someone who wasn't a Christian.

Let's talk about *you* for a minute. Consider the following sce-nario: You've just met a handsome guy with gorgeous eyes at a party. The two of you start talking, and in the course of the con-versation you find out that he's "not really into God." You're dis-appointed, but you still find yourself attracted to this babe in front of you. Before you have time to organize your thoughts, he's uttered those six little words, "Can I take you out some-time?"

How do you handle a situation like that? I think most of us would be tempted to accept his invitation. But by doing so, we would risk getting emotionally attached. Once that happens, it's often too difficult to turn back. That's why it's a good idea to decide not to date unbelievers *before* you're confronted with an uncomfortable situation. Try rehearsing your answer ahead of time, so you don't become tongue-tied.

Still not convinced that it's a bad idea to date people outside your faith? Let's consider the dangers: For one thing, you could begin to compromise your principles. "Do not be misled: 'Bad company corrupts good character,'" according to 1 Corinthians 15:33. A guy without spiritual conviction can tempt you to go places you don't want to go and do things you don't want to do. Also, in the worst-case scenario, your relationship could lead to marriage. You might be thinking you're too strong to be swayed off course, but you'd be surprised how clouded a girl's logic can get when she *really* loves someone.

Some people argue that when you refuse to date unbelievers, you lose opportunities to witness to them. That's not necessarily true. How many people do you know who have actually succeeded at this? Besides, the early stage of dating is not a good time for heavy conversation. Your best chance to witness to a guy is *outside* a romantic/dating relationship.

I'm reminded of a girl who was going through a divorce a few years ago. She had married a non-Christian with the hope that he would convert. He never did, and she ended up being lied to and cheated on during their six years together. After the relationship disintegrated, she talked to my mom about it.

"I don't understand why God allowed me to marry my husband," she cried. "I prayed beforehand and asked the Lord to show me a sign if it wasn't right. I didn't want to make a mistake."

My mom gently reminded her that the "sign" came from the words Jesus spoke in 2 Corinthians 6:14: "Do not be yoked together with unbelievers. For what do righteousness and wickedness have in common? Or what fellowship can light have with darkness?"

The girl had to admit that my mom was right.

Most married Christian couples will tell you that marriage is tough, even in the best of circumstances. How many *more* complications there are when one person has not accepted Christ as his or her personal Savior! That's why it's so important to pray and exercise judgment when it comes to dating. With the Lord's help, you can avoid falling in love with the wrong guy.

your turn

①
Why do you think Jesus emphasized the importance of not being "yoked together with unbelievers"?

②
Name three hazards that can occur when this command is ignored.

③
What would you say to a Christian friend who is interested in dating an unbeliever?

WAITING FOR DATING?

Check It Out!
PHILIPPIANS 1:9-10

"That guy is cute," I whispered to my friend. It was a weekend night, and the two of us were attending a new Bible study for the first time. I must confess that I was checking out the fellas before the session began. Most of them were (yawn) okay-looking, but then *he* came in. This guy was the last person to walk through the door—tall and good-looking, wearing a black shirt and jeans. I thought he was stunning, but not in a drop-dead-gorgeous kind of way. I was attracted to him because he had the kind of "look" that I liked.

It didn't happen overnight, but as I continued to attend the Bible study, my handsome prospect began to notice me. When he called and asked me out, I was *ecstatic* (unbeknownst to him!). I looked forward to our night on the town for a week, and when it arrived I had a really good time. During dinner, we talked openly about God, and I was particularly impressed with the prayer that my date prayed when the meal was served. As far as I was concerned, this guy was a catch! After that enjoyable evening, he asked me out a couple more times. I'd like to be able to tell you that the story had a happy ending, but it didn't. I finally figured out that this guy's interest in me was nothing more than casual and that he was dating other girls. I was *crushed!* It was too late for me to turn back—my heart had already made an investment.

That, my dear friends, is one reason why some people say no to dating. Along with pain and heartache, it can also bring pressure, intimacy, temptation, jealousy, and it can destroy a fine friendship. Dating is fun, but it can also be risky business.

In his book *I Kissed Dating Goodbye*[7], Joshua Harris claims that he has a better idea. He believes that we should hold off on casual romantic encounters in return for something better. More specifically, we should wait for God's plan!

Joshua describes dating as a whimsical phenomenon that lacks purpose or clear destination. It's a short-term arrangement, only serving the needs of the moment. The consensus is, "If the relationship doesn't amount to anything, so what?" Most people date because they want to enjoy the benefits of intimacy without the responsibility of commitment. Dating is a product of our entertainment-driven, "throwaway" American culture.

Intimacy without commitment also awakens emotional and physical desires. As I mentioned earlier, my feelings deepened *after* I went out with the person I was attracted to. If I hadn't spent time alone with him in an intimate setting, his lack of interest wouldn't have hit me so hard.

Ironically, our Bible study covered this topic, long before I went out with my "dream date." The group leader was cautioning us against the hazards of casual dating. He discussed the possibility of broken hearts and damaged friendships. Although he was quick to say that his point of view was not for everyone, he felt that most of us should only go out with someone we would consider marrying.

When the session was over, I approached the teacher and politely disagreed with his position. I told him that I thought dating was important in helping me decide what to look for in a mate. "How else can I get to know a guy if I don't go out with him?" I asked.

The Bible-study teacher explained that there were plenty of opportunities to become acquainted with someone outside of a dating relationship, such as group activities and church functions. In short, he said that anything that keeps me out of an intimate

[7]Multnomah, 1997.

setting with another person is a good idea. The reason for this, he emphasized, is to guard my heart and to avoid the pitfalls that dating can bring. Did I listen to his advice? Not at the time, because I later fell into the trap that he was encouraging me to avoid. I'm now reevaluating my opinion.

Where does the Lord fit into this? Although dating is not mentioned in the Bible, there are many Scriptures that apply to it. One verse that jumps out at me is Proverbs 4:23: "Above all else, guard your heart, for it is the wellspring of life." Notice how the responsibility belongs to us and not God? We can *choose* to direct our minds toward fantasies and make ourselves vulnerable, or we can work at protecting our hearts. It involves self-discipline. Yes, infatuation is a difficult thing to fight, but that doesn't mean we can't control it. If we have a shortcoming in this area, we should call on the Lord for help: "For God is greater than our hearts, and he knows everything" (1 John 3:20).

Another Scripture that is applicable to the dating scene is 1 Thessalonians 4:3-6: "It is God's will that you should be sanctified [holy]: that you should avoid sexual immorality; that each of you should learn to control his own body in a way that is holy and honorable, not in passionate lust like the heathen, who do not know God; and that in this matter no one should wrong his brother or take advantage of him." Let's face it—dating can bring serious temptation. For one thing, most people will only go out with those to whom they're attracted—it's all about chemistry, right? Well, what is chemistry? Isn't it really just sexuality? When a guy and a girl feel this way toward one another, they're bound to encounter some temptation when they spend time alone. The power of sexuality should never be underestimated. That is why some people avoid the dating scene altogether and choose to hang out with groups of friends instead.

Then there are those who believe in courtship, which means that they postpone dating until they feel like they're ready to pursue marriage. When is the right time to begin a courtship? Some common answers are when God gives the go, after college graduation, or upon reaching a certain age. Eventually, when the season is ripe for romance, a guy must first meet the girl's parents. If Mom and Dad approve of the prospective suitor, the young man will begin courting the girl. Then, if all goes as planned, the two of them will fall deeply in love and get married.

Is courtship for you? Perhaps. Pray about it, and talk to your parents as you make your decision.

As for me, I haven't totally given up on dating, but I'm a lot more cautious than I used to be. I have learned that my heart is a vulnerable and delicate entity, greatly in need of my protection. Whenever it tries to run in precarious directions, I do my best to guard it and keep it in full submission to God.

"And this is my prayer: that your love may abound more and more in knowledge and depth of insight, so that you may be able to discern what is best and may be pure and blameless until the day of Christ" (Philippians 1:9-10).

your turn

①

The next time a cute guy shows some interest in you, what are some ways that you can "guard your heart"? (See Proverbs 4:23.)

②

If you are old enough to date, what is the "policy" you have set for yourself?

③

Have you prayed and sought God's will in regard to dating? If not, how about starting right now?

TRUTH OR CONSEQUENCES

Check It Out!
1 TIMOTHY 1:8

What about sex? Should I merely add my voice to the chorus of those who say, "Don't do it before marriage!"? Perhaps, but not without telling you this story: One day I asked a Christian friend why she and her boyfriend weren't sleeping together. She answered me in one simple sentence: "Because God says not to." I liked that reply! Not only did it sum up what the Scriptures had to say, but it got right to the heart of our responsibilities to live a moral life. I have since repeated those words on occasion for those exact reasons.

Why does God tell single people to abstain from sex? Let's analyze this for a moment. Is He trying to spoil our fun and make us miserable? Of course not! His commands in the Bible are for *our* benefit—and they are designed to keep us from creating disastrous situations for ourselves. Consider this: If I decide to jump off a one-thousand-foot cliff, I will die when my body hits the ground. That's a fact. Gravity was designed by God, but not for the purpose of punishing me for my folly. His physical laws govern the universe, and those who defy them are destined to suffer the consequences. So it is with God's moral laws. They, too, are as real and predictable as the principles that govern the world around us.

Let me give you some examples:

True story #1: Kyle wanted to do things his own way. He went through several relationships and slept with each of his girlfriends.

His frivolous lifestyle was fun and exciting—while it lasted. Kyle currently lives in a state of regret over a baby that he fathered and is struggling with child-support payments. Despite Kyle's misery, the baby will be the one who suffers the most for Kyle's mistakes.

True story #2: Amy had an abortion when she was nineteen years old. She is now thirty-four, and although she sought (and received) forgiveness from God, the painful memory lives on. Amy has dealt with a tremendous amount of guilt and remorse over the mistake that she made. With the Lord's help, she is finally working toward putting the past behind her.

True story #3: Kimberlin dated Matt for two years before agreeing to have sex with him. She knew it was wrong, but her decision was easy to rationalize. After all, she and Matt were in love—they would soon be engaged. You can imagine her shock when Matt broke up with her for someone else. Kimberlin is now recovering from a broken heart that took a long time to mend. She admits that the pain wouldn't have been so severe if she hadn't slept with her boyfriend. Now Kimberlin knows that she gave away something precious that she should have saved for her husband.

True story #4: After a party one night, Gina succumbed to having sex with a male friend—just a brief, casual encounter, for the sake of a little fun. Where is Gina now? Currently married, with herpes simplex disease. It is incurable and will plague her for the rest of her life.

What do Kyle, Amy, Kimberlin, and Gina have in common? The answer is easy: None of them thought that their decision to have sex would backfire. They never seriously considered an unplanned pregnancy, a broken heart, or a sexually transmitted disease. These four young people learned the hard way that God's moral laws were set up for their own protection.

Did you know that our Creator formed the moral basis of the universe before He made the heavens and earth? It's true! The concept of right and wrong was in full force before "the beginning." That's what we read in Proverbs 8:22-30, 32-36. These passages, written in first person, refer to "wisdom"—which is seeing things from God's point of view:

> The LORD brought me [wisdom] forth as the first of his works,
> before his deeds of old;
> I was appointed from eternity, from the beginning, before
> the world began.
> When there were no oceans, I was given birth, when there were
> no springs abounding with water;
> before the mountains were settled in place, before the hills,
> I was given birth,
> before he made the earth or its fields or any of the dust
> of the world.
> I was there when he set the heavens in place, when he marked
> out the horizon on the face of the deep,
> when he established the clouds above and fixed securely the
> fountains of the deep,
> when he gave the sea its boundary so the waters would not
> overstep his command, and when he marked out the foundations
> of the earth.
> Then I [wisdom] was the craftsman at his side.
> I was filled with delight day after day, rejoicing always in
> his presence. . . .
> Now then, my sons, listen to me;
> blessed are those who keep my ways.
> Listen to my instruction and be wise; do not ignore it.
> Blessed is the man who listens to me, watching daily at my doors,
> waiting at my doorway.
> For whoever finds me finds life and receives favor from the LORD.
> But whoever fails to find me harms himself; all who hate me love death.

This passage is abundantly clear—and has meaning for each of us. If we live according to God's moral law, we will avoid the awful consequences of sin. We will find "life" and "favor with God." On the other hand, if we defy those laws, pain and heartache are inevitable.

Now that we've examined how premarital sex contradicts

God's moral code, let's explore some of the "sweet benefits of life" that result from following His plan.

The foremost advantage, of course, is having a relationship with Him that is untainted by sexual sin. As you know, sin is a barrier that separates us from God—it is the reason why Jesus came to this earth and died on the cross! Therefore, the only way to experience peace in our relationship with the Lord is by keeping our lives clean . . . and the rewards are enormous.

Here are some other advantages:

- Protection from unnecessary emotional pain
- No guilt!
- No regrettable memories
- Never being used by a guy sexually and then dumped
- Having a reputation that is untarnished by friends' gossip and "locker room stories"
- Avoiding an unplanned pregnancy (and the emotional trauma that goes with it)
- No fear of contacting one of more than twenty sexually transmitted diseases that are now at epidemic proportions
- Having a precious gift (your virginity) to give a future husband
- Maintaining self-respect and dignity

In rereading this list, I'd have to say that it sounds like a win-win situation to me. If you've already fallen into sexual sin, take heart—Jesus offers forgiveness to anyone who sincerely asks for it. Through His grace, you can start again with a clean slate!

Maybe you've already repented, but you've been unable to forgive yourself. Don't become crippled by the past. Put it where it belongs and move forward. If you've truly sought forgiveness for your sins, then God's promise is yours: "I will forgive [your] wickedness and will remember [your] sins no more" (Hebrews 8:12). In other words, "Done!" "Over with!" Therefore, *rejoice,* and see yourself as your heavenly Father sees you—clean, pure, and restored in His grace.

your turn

1

Why did God put wisdom and moral principles into effect before creation?

2

What are some good reasons to abstain from sex until marriage?
(See my list above for clues!)

3

What is the biggest spiritual payoff that comes from following
God's commands?

*"For the wages of sin is death, but the gift of God is eternal life
in Christ Jesus our Lord."*

ROMANS 6:23

ADVANCED
PLANNING

Check It Out!
EPHESIANS 4:22-24

The first time that Brenden and Shari saw each other, they blushed. The embarrassment was more than just an awkward emotion—it was that shy, timid feeling that comes from instant attraction. It didn't take long for a whirlwind romance to develop. After three dates and two trips to Starbucks, the lovebirds shared a passionate kiss. So much for shyness! From then on, Brenden and Shari spent a lot of time hanging out . . . and making out. Although the two teenagers were committed to saving their virginity, they frequently tested the limits of their willpower.

One night after things got a little out of hand, they realized that a decision needed to be made. They had two options: either break up, or put an end to all physical contact. They chose the latter. Interestingly enough, once the passion was removed from their relationship, Brenden and Shari found that they didn't have much to build upon. They bumped along for two more months before calling it quits.

What was wrong with this relationship? Well, for one thing, there was too much emphasis on physical gratification, with no room for personal and spiritual growth.

Also, Brenden and Shari did not honor each other's commitment to purity. If they had perceived one another as a brother and sister in Christ, they would have responded differently. Their goal would have been to guard and protect the other person's righteousness.

Last, and most important, Brenden and Shari did not honor the Lord in their relationship. They were consumed with selfish desires, each focusing on meeting his or her own needs. They also put themselves in a constant battle with temptation, which is never the will of God. He is not impressed by how well two people can resist sexual sin—He wants them to flee from it altogether!

This is why I believe couples shouldn't get too physical in a dating relationship. Passion can cause things to get "too hot to stop" very quickly. Even if standards are high, they can be compromised in the heat of the moment. That's just the way we're wired.

Christian singles have a difficult time controlling their desires for one simple reason, and it has to do with God's plan for marriage. When He "invented" human sexuality, He designed it to have three stages—a prelude, a "fireworks phase" (*boom!*), and a "cool down." He never intended the act to be started and cut short. This is why you shouldn't awaken desires that can't be consummated. Once passions are turned on, they're hard to turn off. Of course, this is irrelevant in a marital relationship—things are *supposed* to get out of control between a husband and a wife.

Even so, Brenden and Shari are not unique. Some Christians believe the Bible is vague in regard to "fooling around." One girl told me that her boyfriend said, "We can't have sex, but we can do everything else." Wrong! Christianity is not about getting as close to the edge as possible. Our priority should be to "flee the evil desires of youth, and pursue righteousness, faith, love and peace, along with those who call on the Lord out of a pure heart" (2 Timothy 2:22). This is unattainable if we're pushing the limits and looking for what we can get away with.

In the case of Brenden and Shari, they quickly learned how "making out" could become a hindrance in their relationship with the Lord. You might even argue that lust became their god for a while. It wasn't until they chose to do what was right that they were able to put things into perspective.

How can you avoid the mistake that this couple made? The best advice that I can give is to point you in the direction of prayer. Talk to God and make a decision *in advance* about what you will NOT do before marriage. Don't wait until you're in the heat of passion to make up your mind. The time is now!

Some of my friends have made similar decisions and have lived up to them. One girl I know made a commitment to avoid situations that might cause her to stumble. As a single young woman, she knows where her weaknesses are, and she doesn't leave herself "wide open" to be tempted. Some other friends of mine, Robert and Ann, dated for five years before they shared their first kiss at the altar. It was a mutual decision and, for them, well worth the sacrifice.

I, too, have established boundaries that I will not cross. Guilt, regret, and temptation are pollutants that gunk up my spiritual life and take my focus off of the Lord. In order to keep the "air" clear, I strive to "seek . . . first the kingdom of God, and his righteousness" (Matthew 6:33, KJV). This involves letting go of my own selfish desires.

What about you? Have you thought about this issue in regard to your own life? What will you do when you're with a guy and you're tempted to compromise? This situation *will* come about, and you need to be prepared. Take some time to think and pray about it now. Meditate on Ephesians 4:22-24, which says, "You were taught, with regard to your former way of life, to put off your old self, which is being corrupted by its deceitful desires; to be made new in the attitude of your minds; and to put on the new self, created to be like God in true righteousness and holiness."

When I reflect upon this passage, the word *purity* comes to mind. Some people equate purity with sexual status, but the verse above teaches that it's a *lifestyle*—a commitment to put God above everything else. This is not burdensome or overwhelming. Those who pursue righteousness will have a fulfilling relationship with Jesus Christ, the Creator of the whole universe! What could be a greater payoff than that? In the long run, any other alternative is harmful and destructive.

Are you ready to give up *everything* for the Lord—including all of your selfish desires? You won't regret that decision!

your turn

①
Why is it difficult for unmarried couples to control their passions?

②
What can you do ahead of time to resist sexual temptation?

③
How does the Bible define purity?

④
What does purity have to do with God's will for your life?

"Blessed are the pure in heart, for they will see God."
MATTHEW 5:8

A COMMON CRIME

Check It Out!
2 TIMOTHY 1:7

Since the majority of you will be dating soon, if you're not already, it would be wise for us to discuss something that may be very important to you in the future. I'm referring specifically to the issue of date rape. Most people assume that it will never happen to them. However, the reality is that date rape is a serious threat, and girls who are between the ages of sixteen and twenty-five are at the highest risk for it.[8] Does this mean that you should live in fear? No, but it's a good idea to be informed. One of the most effective defensive strategies is knowing how to stay out of danger.

Check out these statistics: According to the Federal Bureau of Investigation, 61 percent of rape victims are under the age of eighteen, yet only one out of every ten cases is reported to law enforcement authorities.[9] This means that the majority of rapists are never punished for their crimes. They are free to assault again.

Here's something that's even more disturbing: When 1,700 junior-high students in an inner city were questioned about the subject of rape, 25 percent of the boys and 16 percent of the girls

[8]Bureau of Justice Statistics, Criminal Victimization of the United States, U.S. Department of Justice, Washington, D.C., 1991.

[9]Thomas, Karen, "Who are the Child Molesters among Us?" *USA TODAY*, 12 March 2002.

said that they thought rape was acceptable if the man had spent money on the woman.[10] Also, 65 percent of the boys and 47 percent of the girls said that it is okay for a man to force sex on a woman if the couple has been dating for at least six months.[11] This survey, conducted by the Rhode Island Rape Crisis Center, reveals how conditioned many girls and boys are to the idea that sexual abuse isn't all that bad.

These findings are incomprehensible. How could anyone, especially a girl, believe that forced sex is tolerable under *any* circumstance? Yet 41 percent of the students who were interviewed said that rape is justified in certain situations. I wonder if they would feel the same if they themselves were the ones being victimized.

Focus on the Family, a ministry dedicated to the preservation of the family, receives approximately 250,000 letters and phone calls each month. Some of these come from girls who were sexually abused during adolescence by boys they were dating. These young women bear the emotional wounds of betrayal and degradation.

Maybe you've suffered this trauma in your own life. If you have, my heart goes out to you. I pray that God will heal your pain and give you a sense of peace and renewal. The psalmist David wrote: "The righteous cry out, and the Lord hears them; he delivers them from all their troubles. The Lord is close to the brokenhearted and saves those who are crushed in spirit" (Psalm 34:17-18). I hope that this Scripture will be a source of encouragement to you. May I also suggest that you seek out a Christian counselor, physician, or pastor? It's healthy to talk about your feelings. One girl who went to therapy gave this response: "It was *so* helpful. For the first time, I felt like [the rape] wasn't this awful secret I had to live with." If you've been violated in the past, I hope that you will seek help. It's essential to your recovery. Finally, I strongly urge you to report any sexual abuse to the police or to a responsible

---

[10]Lewis, Claude, "Date Rape Is OK, Grade Schoolers Say," *Philadelphia Inquirer,* 4 May 1988.

[11] Ibid.

adult. You'll feel safer if your abuser is caught, and you may also be saving other girls from a similar tragedy.

Whether or not you've been a victim of rape in the past, you can take action *now* for the future. Let's go over some strategies.

One important principle is to use good judgment in the company you keep. You've probably heard stories about girls who went on dates and ended up being drugged and taken advantage of. One female victim said that she went on a date, expecting to have some innocent fun. Instead, she was drugged and molested in the back of the guy's car. "You don't know people as well as you think you do," she warned.

As this young woman continued to share her story, she admitted that she had only known the guy for several hours. She also had a couple of drinks that night, which left her vulnerable and unguarded. I'm not saying that this girl caused her own misfortune, but she could have done more to protect herself.

What about you? Do you take precautions when you go out? What about the guys you hang with? Are they committed Christians—people you trust? I know that there's no guarantee of safety, but it's wise to be selective about anyone you spend time with

Your choice of activities is important, too. A word about the "party scene": Despite the moral concerns about drinking and using drugs, there's also the issue of safety. A person who gets high or intoxicated is sending a message to a potential rapist. That message spells "VICTIM." Also, partying causes you to lose your sense of judgment. The Scripture says: "Therefore do not be foolish, but understand what the Lord's will is. Do not get drunk on wine, which leads to debauchery. Instead, be filled with the Spirit" (Ephesians 5:17-18). If you're unsure about the meaning of the word "debauchery," here is the dictionary definition: "To cause (someone) to become corrupt in virtue, especially with regard to drinking or sexual behavior." Bottom line: There are a number of reasons to stay away from booze and drugs, including your own safety. Don't lose your edge!

Unfortunately, even if you avoid mind-altering substances

and follow the rules, you can still encounter a dangerous situation. The world is evil, and bad things do happen to good people. For this reason, you might want to take a self-defense class. Also, the Pregnancy Resource Center will provide you with antirape education. You can locate their Web site at http://www.pregnancy-centers.org.

Finally, I would be remiss if I didn't mention the most powerful defense that you have against violence: *prayer*. The Scriptures tell us that there is a battle going on in the world. It is known as spiritual warfare. Satan is a real being, in spite of what you may have heard, and his primary objective is to entice you and me to do things that are wrong. Then the consequences come crashing down on us, and Satan has destroyed another soul. It happens millions of times every year. Peter said, "Be self-controlled and alert. Your enemy the devil prowls around like a roaring lion looking for someone to devour" (1 Peter 5:8).

And John said, "The one who is in you [Jesus] is greater than the one who is in the world [Satan]" (1 John 4:4). You do not have to be victimized by the forces of evil.

Pray for the Lord's protection. Ask Him to give you discernment regarding the people that you hang around and the places you go. Trust Him to help you make wise decisions.

As long as there is sin in the world, the threat of violence and hate crimes is not going to go away. The good news is that we do not have to live in fear. We can move forward with courage, for "God has not given us a spirit of fear, but of power and of love and of a sound mind" (2 Timothy 1:7, NKJV).

your turn

①

What are some effective defense strategies against violence? Would you:

- Go out with a guy whose morals are different from yours?
- Enter a guy's home alone with him?
- Get into a car with a guy whom you just met (or don't know very well)?

If you answered yes to any of the above questions, then you are too trusting.
Don't be a risk-taker!

②

**Have you learned to listen to the little voice that warns you when
you are about to do something unwise or wrong? It's your conscience,
and it will guard you if you heed it!**

SOUND OFF

Check It Out!
JOB 34:4

For a balanced view on dating, I thought it might be helpful to get a male perspective. I decided to track down some guys from my church's youth group and see what they had to say about girls and relationships.

I arranged to meet the guys at church on a Sunday afternoon. I brought my cassette recorder, along with some American "dude food": double burgers, fries, and Cokes. After we chowed down, I asked the guys a variety of questions, on everything from cosmetics to courtship, and recorded their responses. As you will see, they were direct and candid in sharing their opinions.

Before you read what my four friends had to say, I'd like to introduce each of them to you:

Name: Justin Hodgson
Age: 16
Favorite subject in school: lunch
Favorite sport: snowboarding
Favorite food: bratwurst

Name: Jon Ramirez
Age: 18
Favorite subject in school: English
Favorite sport: basketball
Favorite food: double hamburgers

Name: Chris Camping
Age: 17
Favorite subject in school: physics
Favorite sport: track and field
Favorite food: tuna casserole

Name: Joshua Jacobs
Age: 17
Favorite subject in school: history
Favorite sport: basketball
Favorite food: Skittles

❶ *What qualities are you looking for in a girl?*

Justin: She would need to be someone who is truly devoted to God. The only other thing that matters to me is being able to share a deep friendship.

Josh: I'd want her to have a good walk with the Lord and to have a strong, Christian family background. Obviously, she would need to be attractive. Oh! . . . and I guess she would need to like me!

Chris: Attractive, not only physically, but also mentally and socially. I wouldn't be interested in someone who acted like a ditz. Also, a good walk with the Lord is essential. Some other traits that I like are a nice personality and a sense of humor. A little bit of a challenge doesn't hurt, either. I can be moody sometimes, and I like a girl who won't put up with it.

Jon: I want a girl to be serious about her Christian faith. It's important to me that she goes to church and has a desire to grow and learn. If she's good-looking, that's fine, but I don't really care about physical beauty. Personality matters more to me.

❷ *What do you like most about girls?*

Chris: A lot of girls are good conversationalists! I'm a talkative person, and I can have some really good in-depth conversations with girls.

Jon: Girls tend to be comforting and understanding. If I'm going through a tough time, it's easy for me to talk to them about it.

Josh: I think girls have better attention spans than guys do. I've also noticed that they're better listeners, they're more rational, and they care more about people as individuals.

❸ What turns you off about girls?

Chris: Clingy girls are a turnoff. They get mad at their boyfriends for going out with the guys, which isn't cool.

Justin: Superficiality! I've observed that most girls are superficial in the way they look and act—they don't like to be themselves around people.

Jon: I don't like girls who are boring and too serious. They should lighten up and be more outgoing.

Josh: Inappropriate use of language—not just vulgarity and cussing, but also with speech patterns. People are judged and identified by how they communicate, and that's a big deal. The way a girl carries herself when she speaks is important.

Another thing that bothers me is when girls won't express their opinions. It's the whole conformist thing--going along with what everyone else is saying or doing. That's a big turnoff.

❹ When it comes to girls' hair, clothes, and makeup, what drives you insane?

Jon: I don't like trendfollowers—girls who look like clones. My advice is, "Be yourself, and don't wear trendy clothes and makeup."

Justin: It bothers me when girls won't go into the water at the beach or a swim party because they're wearing makeup. I mean, why do girls go to the beach if they won't go in the water? There aren't too many things that bug me about makeup and stuff, but this is one of them.

Josh: Obsessive-compulsive disorder with makeup! Justin said earlier that he doesn't like superficiality. I think that wearing too much makeup is a form of being superficial. If a guy marries a girl, he's gonna wake up to her hair and makeup not being perfect.

There's a lot of cute girls at my school, and sometimes they oversleep in the morning and don't have time to put their makeup on. Their parents make them come to class anyway. It's kind of a shocker, because a girl will say, "Hi, Josh," and I hardly recognize her.

I also don't like red lipstick. There's a girl in my class who wears it, and when I look at her, all I see are lips!

To me, there's nothing more beautiful than a girl who feels like she doesn't need makeup and doesn't want it. A little is okay, but natural is best.

Chris: Trendy blue eye shadow! A subtle effect is okay, but some girls look like they have a second pair of eyes, or like they're wearing blue sunglasses. I think that's revolting.

I agree with Josh: A little makeup is fine, but natural is best.

In regard to clothes, here's a tip: Guys may like it when girls dress sexy, but we don't respect them for it. Clothes can make or break a girl in how a guy perceives her. If a girl dresses modestly, it leaves more to the imagination and keeps a guy wondering. Personally, I like it when a girl wears a nice-fitting pair of jeans.

❺ Why do some girls seem to get all the guys?

Josh: From what I've observed in public school, there are two reasons why some girls get all the guys: One, the girls are good-looking and really nice. Two, they are good-looking and morally decadent. Some of them just want to "hook up" short-term and don't care about their reputations.

I admit that a lot of guys concentrate too much on outward appearance. I know it isn't fair, but that's the way we are. I think a lot of relationships don't last for this reason. For instance, a guy will pursue a girl because she's cute, but then he has to start communicating with her. He soon realizes that outward appearance doesn't matter, but he'll go out and repeat the cycle again.

Chris: A lot of guys are attracted to the "girl-next-door" type—someone who is sweet and genuine. Good morals are really important.

Jon: Girls who are confident and outgoing seem to attract a lot of attention. Guys like to be around girls who have fun personalities.

Justin: I've noticed that it's not always true that the hottest girls get all the guys. Personality goes further. Good looks go a long way, but not as far as being friendly. Some chicks have a lot of success because they're just awesome people.

❻ What is the best way for a girl to get a guy's attention?

Jon: When a guy is attracted to a girl, it's really hard for him to ask her out. It would be easier if she helped him out. If she came up and initiated some conversation, it would alleviate some of the pressure.

Josh: If you like someone, you have to eventually say it or show it. Here's one way to get the point across: If a guy offers you something, take it! For instance, if it's cold, and he offers you his jacket, you should accept it. It doesn't matter if you don't need the jacket, or even if you're hotter than all blazes. Take it anyway, and drape it over your arm. This is important, because it represents one of the first contacts. If you refuse what a guy is offering, it kind of rejects him in some way. It makes it more difficult for him the next time.

Chris: Find common ground with the guy. If you both like drama, or the same music band, talk about it with him. If he's interested in you, he'll take it from there.

❼ What would you think about a girl asking you out?

Chris: I might find that a little weird. I still believe that a guy should initiate, but a girl can help by making it easier for him.

Jon: I wouldn't have a problem with her asking me to a school function or something. It might get the ball rolling for me to ask her out the next time.

Justin: Traditionally, a guy is supposed to do the asking, so I might find that a little strange. It would depend on the girl, though. If I felt a connection with her, I'd probably just go along with it.

Josh: This just happened to me a few days ago. One of my friends told me that "so and so" liked me, and I never knew the girl existed. It was an awkward situation, because I wasn't attracted to her, and she was being way too aggressive. She was also getting our mutual friend to be aggressive, too. My friend was asking me questions like, "Josh, why don't you take her off campus for lunch?"

So, to answer the question, I don't see any harm in a girl asking me out, as long as she doesn't come on too strong. If I'm attracted to her, I'll respond.

❽ *What should a girl never do to get a guy?*

Chris: A girl should *never* get her best friend to pressure the guy! Also, she shouldn't talk to her fifteen closest friends about him. Those fifteen friends will go up to the guy, one at a time, and ask him a bunch of questions. That's really annoying! A girl should keep her friends out of the loop. Another thing a girl should never do is compromise her morals.

Jon: She shouldn't play mind games to win someone's affections. For example, if a guy is into roller blading, she shouldn't tell him that she likes to do that sort of thing if she doesn't. That causes problems.

Josh: My advice is for a girl not to be too aggressive. If she's always in contact with the guy whom she likes, it can get really uncomfortable for him. This turns off a relationship real fast.

Justin: When a girl is attracted to a guy, she shouldn't try to get information from his friends. That's a big mistake. She should just be direct with the guy.

❾ *What do you think about girls who chase after guys?*

Josh: The way I see it, if a guy likes a girl, he's gonna stop running. There's never a reason to chase anyone. From a guy's perspective, it's flattering when a girl does this, but it doesn't accomplish what she wants. It ruins the hopes of anything developing in the future.

Jon: It's harmless unless the chasing turns into stalking. For example, if a girl drives past a guy's house because she has nothing better to do, there's something wrong with that.

Chris: If a guy tells a girl that he's not interested, and she keeps coming after him, it gets really annoying. It's also degrading to the girl to lower herself like that.

Justin: It's okay if the girl is just doing it to have fun and not to get a boyfriend out of it. If she just wants to be flirty, that's fine. I don't see any harm in it.

⑩ Is double/group dating better than one-on-one?

Justin: I think that double-dating is more fun than a one-on-one situation. It's awesome to go out with another "rad" couple. It also takes away the temptation that you might feel in an intimate setting. It looks better to parents, too, when they see you going out with other people.

Chris: Dating can bring lots of pressure, so I think that going out with other couples is a good idea. I have done this before, and it's really fun. The more people who are there, the more interesting conversations you can have. You don't have to deal with the lag time.

Jon: Group dating definitely keeps you in check, and it helps with temptation. However, there are times when you want to be alone with a person, and times when you want to have friends around.

Josh: It's okay, but it can be jarring sometimes. If the other couple is showing more affection, or if they are arguing—or vice versa— it can be awkward.

⑪ What do you think about courtship?

Justin: I don't think that you can find what you're looking for if you stick with one person. In order to recognize what you like and don't like, you need to date around a little bit. That's what dating is for.

Josh: I saw a documentary on courtship, and I think it has positive and negative aspects. It makes sense to talk to a girl's parents and get to know her family. That's important. Also, courtship takes the place of casual dating, which is good in a lot of ways. The downside is that it kind of ruins the fun aspect of going out and getting to know someone. It's like being married with none of the perks. I'm in favor of starting out as friends with a girl, and finding out who she is. I'd like to discover, in a natural way, if I could fall in love with her.

Chris: I don't agree with courtship at all. I think that a couple needs casual one-on-one time to get to know each other. Also, they should get to know each other's parents on a deeper level before going out for the sake of marriage.

Personally, I want to have a serious relationship that goes the distance, but I don't want to be bound prematurely. I don't want to go from hardly knowing a girl to becoming "engaged," so to speak.

Jon: I prefer the idea of just having a long-term relationship that leads to marriage. A guy and girl can still follow some of the guidelines of courtship, like waiting to kiss, but they don't have to be so strict.

⑫ *What do you think about kissing?*

Josh: Once a guy kisses a girl, that's all he thinks about. Courtship is good in the sense that couples don't kiss and get physical before marriage. They're able to concentrate on other aspects of their relationship.

Justin: I don't see anything wrong with kissing, but it's important to establish physical boundaries in the relationship. I think it's a good idea to agree to never be alone together.

Chris: I haven't kissed a girl yet. Ideally, I would like my first kiss to be with the person I'm going to marry. I want my first kiss to be really special.

⑬ *What is the best way to avoid sexual temptation?*

Josh: Set limits in your mind while you're thinking clearly! Don't wait until you succumb to hormones—the boundary will just keep going farther and farther.

You also shouldn't put yourself in a tempting situation, like sitting in a dark room with someone, watching a movie. Make sure there are other people around.

Chris: In addition to creating mental boundaries, you should discuss the issue with whomever you're dating. Make it clear that you don't want to go any farther than the limit that you've set. Tell the person that you respect him and his future spouse.

Justin: I have a girlfriend, and when we started going out, we talked about this subject. We created standards for our relationship. In order to stay true to them, we make sure that we're always with someone, and we're not alone together. Promise rings are a good idea, too—I gave my girlfriend one that matches mine.

Jon: Respect the other person enough to know your boundaries. You should also respect their future spouse. You might have to look that guy's wife in the eye someday, and you don't want to be ashamed of anything. A good question to ask yourself is, "How would I feel if my soul mate had already had an experience on that level?" It would be really sad to not be able to share that first time with my spouse.

⓮ What do you feel is God's standard for you in regard to dating?

Jon: I think God wants me to be up front and direct with whomever I'm going out with. He wants me to communicate my morals and then abide by them.

Chris: Up to this point, I've only gone out with one girl for a month. I want a relationship to go somewhere, so I'm not really into casual dating. It doesn't make sense to get to know a girl and her parents, and then to break up.

Eventually I hope to meet someone that I'd like to marry. I hope that she will strengthen me in my faith, just as I will strengthen her. It would be important to base our relationship on the Lord and to spend time with Him—not just independently—but as a couple.

Josh: God expects me to live up to the standards that I've set for myself. He trusts me to choose the right person to date and to hold true to my convictions.

Justin: The Lord wants me to use discernment. If I started dating someone who didn't live by God's principles, I would feel a need to back away from that relationship.

♡

There you have it—straight talk from four perceptive young men! I hope that you found their insights to be helpful and informative. You may not have agreed with everything they said, but at least they got you thinking!

> "Let us discern for ourselves what is right; let us learn together what is good."
>
> JOB 34:4

Let's talk about YOU!

Everlasting Beauty   And It's Worth It!   Stressed Out!
Don't Give Up   A Hunger for Acceptance
Nothing More than Feelings   You Can Be Who You Want to Be
A King's Kid

A KING'S KID

Check It Out!
LAMENTATIONS 3:22-23

Have you ever stopped to consider how valuable you are to God? The Bible tells us that He created us in His own image and that we rank just a little lower than the angels. That's pretty significant, don't you think?

As a demonstration of His great love for us, God sent His very own Son, Jesus, to die for our sins. My pastor often emphasized that Jesus would have paid that penalty even if I were the *only person who ever lived.* We have been given glory and honor and the gift of eternal life! How special and valuable we are in the eyes of the Creator!

You would think that this assurance would cause a person to feel pretty confident, wouldn't you? But all too often, that's not the case. Millions of people suffer from feelings of worthlessness and insignificance. This low opinion of one's self has the capacity to strip away all confidence and paralyze a person from accomplishment. The result: insecurity, discontentment, and in extreme cases, clinical depression.

Dr. Smiley Blanton, a famous psychiatrist of the twentieth century, used to say that the most common problem he was presented with in counseling was low self-esteem. His patients suffered tremendous feelings of inadequacy that led them to seek professional

help. Dr. Blanton, who was knowledgeable of the Bible, always referred his patients to the second-greatest commandment: "Love
your neighbor as yourself" (Matthew 22:39).

"There it is!" this doctor would say. "Love is the answer to all
human ills. The Bible says—" and he would thrust the book right
into his patient's hands— "that you can't love anyone if you despise
and downgrade yourself. There it is, right there. See? Right there!"

If God commands us to "love our neighbor as ourselves," then
that must mean that He expects us to hold ourselves in high regard. Obviously, this does not mean with pride or conceit, but
rather with a great deal of respect. In other words, if you have a
good self-concept, you'll be able to quit focusing on yourself—*Do I
look okay? Do people like me?*—and focus on others.

Do you have a positive self-image? If you don't, you're not
alone. Millions of people, and probably the majority of kids at your
school, are in the same boat. It's a shame, because nobody is born
with this inferior mind-set. Young children don't fret about who is
smarter or prettier.

When a healthy baby enters the world, he doesn't worry about
whether he's good enough; he assumes his parents love him. As
far as anyone can tell, this little bundle has a strong ego (and a
strong set of lungs!). As time progresses, however, a child's high
opinion of himself can be damaged. A critical parent—an over-
bearing sibling—other children who tease and ridicule—all of
these forces can cause a youngster to question his value.

Another destructive contributor is the tendency to compare
our weaknesses with the strengths of others. Ever since I was a little
girl, I've heard my dad utter this simple phrase: "Comparison is the
root of all inferiority." It's true that we form damaging conclusions
by measuring our worth against someone else. That's what spurs
these thoughts:

- *I'm not pretty enough.*
- *I lack intelligence.*
- *I'm uncoordinated.*
- *I'm a failure.*

Here's an example of how this can occur: At a church function awhile back, I spotted a guy that I was attracted to. To my delight, he initiated a conversation with me, and I caught him glancing my way a few times when he thought I wasn't looking. *This is great,* I said to myself, *the attraction must be mutual!*

Boy, did I get the wind taken out of my sails! At the next function, a girl showed up who hadn't been there the week before. She was—how shall I put it—well endowed, and she was wearing an outfit that emphasized her shapely figure. The next thing I knew, Romeo was enthusiastically trying to engage her in conversation. I cringed as I heard the two of them talking and laughing and flirting with each other. It made me feel totally insignificant! As I drove away that night, the devil clobbered me over the head all the way home. My mind was spilling over with self-loathing thoughts that tore into my psyche. It was very upsetting! Eventually, the Lord helped me to reestablish my confidence, but the healing process didn't happen overnight.

All of us experience doubts and fears at some point—it's part of being human. There are a number of people, however, who go through life feeling this way. They are in a constant state of defeat, and they end up "crawling" instead of standing tall and proud. My heart goes out to these dear ones, because I understand this kind of pain.

So, what can we do to overcome feelings of self-doubt?

First, stop comparing yourself to other people! Today I was reading an article that was written by a woman who didn't like her hair. She began by comparing her unwanted tresses to Jennifer Aniston's. As many of you know, Jennifer is an actress who is *known* for her flawless mane. Why would anyone punish herself by comparing her hair to someone else's, especially when the other person's gorgeous mane doesn't represent the norm?

Learn to accept yourself as God made you, then make the most of your *own* attributes!

Second, get a deep sense of the presence of God in your life. It's hard to stay focused on yourself when you're filling your mind with spiritual things. You can do this by praying, reading your Bible, and getting involved in some type of ministry. Giving to and caring for others is wonderful medicine! This is the best way to get beyond fear and a sense of failure. I guarantee that it will have a healthy effect on your self-esteem, too!

Third, recognize yourself as a "King's kid"—a child of our Father in heaven. If God considers you valuable enough to call you His own daughter, then you must be pretty special indeed.

Let me close with the words of David, written so eloquently in the book of Psalms:

> "For you created my inmost being; you knit me together in my mother's womb. I praise you because I am fearfully and wonderfully made; your works are wonderful, I know that full well. My frame was not hidden from you when I was made in the secret place. When I was woven together in the depths of the earth, your eyes saw my unformed body. All the days ordained for me were written in your book before one of them came to be" (Psalm 139:13-16).

your turn

1

Have you struggled with self-esteem issues in the past? If so, examine your life and see if you can grasp a specific cause for your feelings of inferiority.

2

How could learning to accept yourself enable you to reach out to other people?

3

Doubt and fear are major hindrances to a person's ego. Think of a problem that intimidates you and ask God to help you take some action against it. This is sure to increase your confidence.

DON'T GET DISSED

Check It Out!
<small>PROVERBS 3:3-4</small>

Take a moment to think about some of the popular students at your school. Why are they at the top of the heap? Are they friendly, outgoing, attractive, fashionable, funny? How about the unpopular students? Do they dress weird or try too hard to get attention? Are they so eager to make friends that they turn people off? Do they seem angry and distant?

The purpose of this chapter is not to turn you into a campus queen but to keep the opposite from happening. Popularity is superficial, but no one likes to be snubbed, either. It's painful to be teased or dissed by peers, yet many teens make mistakes that bring ridicule upon themselves. I've seen it happen time and again.

One of the most common errors is when teens *allow* others to treat them with disrespect. Once that begins, it can have a snowball effect! When I was in junior high, I overheard some guys asking a girl for sexual favors. Instead of putting a stop to it, she tried to hide her uneasiness by joking around. Knowing that they could get away with it, the guys began harassing her on a regular basis. I could tell that the poor girl didn't like their taunting, but she felt powerless to do anything about it.

She should have politely stood up for herself when the very first comment was made. If that didn't work, she might have notified a school official. That kind of sexual harrassment is actually illegal, and a person does not have to take it. The most important thing to remember in a moment like this is not to reveal extreme irritation and explosive anger. When the bullies see that they are getting to the victim, the "fun" is only beginning.

A few years ago, a friend came up with a variation of my name that I found unflattering. With a courteous tone, I asked him not to refer to me like that again. It has now been three years, and I haven't heard it since. Most of the time, that's all it takes to discourage a person from being obnoxious. It also shows that you respect yourself, which is a key ingredient to being treated well.

One more mistake is the tendency to try too hard to win someone's approval. When I was in ninth grade, I transferred to a different school. As the new girl on campus, I was eager to make friends and find my niche. In order to accomplish this, I made it a point to learn the names of my fellow classmates. When I passed someone whom I recognized, I would smile and greet the person by name—a nice gesture, don't you think? Well, I quickly learned that this was *not* working in my favor. I was trying too hard to fit in, and people were picking up on it. Moral of the story: It's good to be friendly, but don't go overboard.

There *is* such a thing as being too eager for friends. Others might even take advantage of you by getting you to do their homework, to keep giving them money, or to lie or steal for them.

What does God have to say about our relationships with others? The book of Proverbs is filled with words of wisdom that help us to see things from God's point of view. One of my favorite passages is found in chapter 2. It reads, "For the LORD gives wisdom, and from his mouth come knowledge and understanding. He holds victory in store for the upright, he is a shield to those whose walk is blameless, for he guards the course of the just and protects the way of his faithful ones. Then you will understand what is right and just and fair—every good path. For wisdom will enter your heart, and knowledge will be pleasant to your soul. Discretion will protect you, and understanding will guard you" (vv. 6-11).

This Scripture can be applied to every aspect of our lives—including the way we deal with others.

Wisdom is what motivates us to say and do the right thing. It's what keeps us from making mistakes with people and what drives us to be the best that we can be. Wisdom, of course, comes from God.

A wise and discerning girl can usually avoid being made a laughingstock by her peers. She will think before she speaks, display a friendly disposition, and communicate respect for everyone, including herself. Someone of this mind-set has a good chance of being well liked and accepted. As for the people you know who are being teased or who don't have many friends, be sure to show kindness to them. I once picked on a guy because I saw other kids doing it. Wrong move! Proverbs 24:23 says, "These are also the sayings of the wise: To show partiality in judging is not good." Everyone deserves to be treated with dignity, regardless of what your friends might think. Always treat people the way that *you* want to be treated. "Let love and faithfulness never leave you; bind them around your neck, write them on the tablet of your heart. Then you will win favor and a good name in the sight of God and man" (Proverbs 3:3-4).

your turn

❶
Where do knowledge and wisdom come from? How can we achieve them?

❷
Name one way that you can be more wise in your interactions with others.

NOTHING MORE THAN FEELINGS

Check It Out!
2 CORINTHIANS 10:5

Have you ever been bummed one day and happy the next? Have you ever felt strongly about something and then suddenly changed your mind? Have you ever been attracted to a guy and later decided he was a loser?

Each of these three questions has one thing in common: They all relate to how you feel. Interestingly, my dad wrote a book about this subject and titled it *Emotions—Can You Trust Them?*[12]. Obviously, the answer to his question is, "No, you can't trust the way you feel." Emotions spin on a dime, and they are extremely unreliable. They are also deceptive, especially in the teen years when hormones are flying high.

As females, we tend to be more in touch with our feelings than our male counterparts are. We're more apt to cry at sad movies and experience mood swings. Premenstrual syndrome (PMS) can account for some of this. One girl told me that during the week before her period, she often cries and questions whether or not she has any real friends. Afterwards, just like clockwork, her self-image

[12]Regal, 1980.

improves and the world looks better. Not everybody is this volatile, but all of us are influenced to some extent by hormonal changes in our bodies. The wonderful thing is that we do not have to be controlled by them! Understanding and knowledge can help us to take charge of our emotions.

One of the signs of maturity is the ability (and the willingness) to overrule feelings with *reason*. This might lead you to hang in there when you feel like quitting . . . to put the brakes on sexual desire when you feel like giving in . . . to bite your tongue when you feel like yelling . . . to save your money when you feel like blowing it . . . to put someone else's needs above your own. These are mature responses that can't occur when emotions are in charge.

There's a Scripture, 2 Corinthians 10:5, that speaks to this subject: "We take captive every thought to make it obedient to Christ." When I meditate on this verse, the word "self-control" comes to mind. You might remember that this is one of the fruits of the Spirit in Galatians 5:22. When God is at work in our lives, He will produce the fruit of self-discipline within us. It is a gift for those who seek Him.

Allow me to illustrate: Crista was sixteen years old when she began dating Darren. Their relationship was a roller coaster from the start. Yes, there was a definite attraction between them, but Crista's inability to control her temper was an ongoing problem. Whenever she and Darren had a fight, Crista would slam the phone down in his ear or the door in his face. She wrote hostile letters with the cruelest of intentions; she shouted and cursed. Crista didn't just lack self-control; she was *out of control!* Darren finally bailed on the relationship, probably in an attempt to preserve his sanity.

Ten years have passed since that stormy era, and Crista now has a mature relationship with another guy. When asked to what she attributes this positive change, Crista credits the Lord—and a considerable amount of spiritual growth. She admits that during her high school era, she was a "watered-down Christian," consumed with her own selfish needs and desires. Once Crista allowed God to take control of her personality and her circumstances, some beautiful changes began to occur. The most apparent was the ability to manage her anger.

This is one example of how spiritual maturity can affect a person's behavior. When our lives are rooted in Christ, we have a greater capacity to manage our emotions.

Of course, even with God's help, our feelings will still fluctuate. This is part of the human condition. Sometimes people will make us so angry that we want to clobber them. Fear, fatigue, and hormonal changes can wreak havoc on our ability to stay calm. At times like these, we need to draw upon the Lord for His strength.

Just this past week, I spoke to a large group of women at a church in Indiana. As you can imagine, I was pretty nervous. Thoughts of "What if?" were attacking my confidence level. Shortly before I was scheduled to speak, I went to the rest room. While I was adjusting my skirt, this sentence came to my mind: "Allow knowledge to override your feelings." It was like a lightbulb flashed in my mind! At that point I took control of my anxious thoughts and replaced them with messages of courage and strength. And it worked! I had a renewed sense of confidence, and I made it through the speech without a hitch. I'm certain that God gave me that encouraging sentence to help me overcome my uneasiness. Without His influence, I probably would have been a lot more tense at the podium.

That simple message of letting knowledge override feelings can be applied to other situations as well. For instance, if there is ever a time when our emotions go haywire, it's when we're attracted to someone, right? We can't wait to see the guy, and our heart beats faster when we're around him. If the attraction is mutual, well . . . need I say more? It truly is a state of euphoria!

At some point, though, a reality check comes into play. Either our knight in shining armor falls off his white horse, or we simply return to a degree of normalcy. Either way, what goes up must come down—we can't live in the clouds forever. Even couples who have been happily married for years will tell you that they regularly go through peaks and valleys in their relationship. There is a definite swing to the emotions of love, just as with every other aspect of feelings. What holds a couple steady for a lifetime of marriage, then, is not the consistency of exhilaration; it is a commitment of the *will* that overrides fickle feelings. Especially in a marital context, emotions cannot be trusted.

You may have noticed that your relationship with the Lord travels through ups and downs also. At times you may feel spiritual passion, and other times you may feel nothing at all. This, too, is typical of us all. If your faith is grounded in the Word and not on feelings, it won't unravel during the blasé periods.

So, enjoy the moments of exhilaration when they come, but don't get hooked on them. Take charge of your emotions, and when it comes time to do the right thing, don't allow your feelings to lead you astray. This is the best way to experience some of life's *greatest* emotions—peace and contentment.

your turn

❶
Why are feelings often unreliable?

❷
Name a time when you displayed emotional immaturity. What could you have done differently?

❸
What does it mean to "take captive every thought to make it obedient to Christ"? (See 2 Corinthians 10:5.)

STRESSED OUT!

Check It Out!
MATTHEW 11:28-29

A while ago I ran into my friend Susan at church on Sunday. It had been a long time since we'd seen each other, and we had a lot of catching up to do. We stood and chatted for about thirty minutes after the service. Finally, Susan mentioned that she was late picking up her daughter from Sunday school. I decided to go with her so we could finish our conversation.

We continued to talk and giggle as we made our way to the children's department. But before we could get there, her daughter, Caitlyn, burst through the double doors. She had been watching for her mother through the window and was very emotional. The little girl cried uncontrollably as she latched onto her mother's knees. A Sunday school teacher followed closely behind.

"What's wrong?" asked Susan.

"Caitlyn was worried that you weren't going to pick her up," said the teacher with a smile.

Susan knelt down and hugged her daughter. "It's all right, honey," she said.

Caitlyn was still consumed with anxiety. Between short breaths, she tried to voice her frustration. "You said you were going to pick me up after church," she sobbed. "You didn't come."

As I stood there taking in all this drama, I couldn't help but think that Caitlyn was overreacting. It seemed irrational for a seven-year-old to be upset over something so insignificant. I tried to ease Caitlyn's distress by applying some common sense. "You know your mommy would never leave you," I explained. "She's just a little late, that's all." I waited for Susan to reinforce my words, but she didn't say anything. She just held her daughter and gently stroked her hair.

When Caitlyn regained control of her emotions, her mother stood up and took her by the hand. Thanking the Sunday school teacher, Susan dabbed Caitlyn's eyes and began leading her out to the car.

As I walked along beside them, I admired the way Susan handled the situation. She could have made Caitlyn feel childish or tried to reason with her. Instead, she just wrapped her arms around her daughter in an expression of love. That's all Caitlyn needed to overcome her distress.

Not long after that, I found myself in my *own* emotional turmoil. I was fearful about something that wasn't grounded on any evidence. Friends and family told me that I was probably overreacting. I knew I was, too, but I couldn't overcome my anxiety. Then I took the matter to the Lord in prayer.

"Dear God," I prayed. "I know I'm probably not making a lot of sense, but would You please comfort me? That's what I need right now . . . to feel You hold me with the assurance that everything will be okay."

Instantly, the picture came to my mind of Susan and Caitlyn in front of the Sunday school building. Just knowing the Lord was providing me with the same security helped me to put away my fear.

Life is full of day-to-day stresses—everything from stubbing your toe to the unthinkable can happen. I believe Jesus cares about what bothers us, whether it's valid or not. He created us, so He understands our feelings. He even told us: "Come to me, all you who are weary and burdened, and I will give you rest. Take my yoke upon you and learn from me, for I am gentle and humble in heart, and you will find rest for your souls" (Matthew 11:28-29).

Notice that there are no restrictions mentioned? That verse

encourages you to bring your cares to Him regardless of what they are. Whether you're facing the loss of a grandparent or just struggling with mood swings, the Lord knows and understands. And here's a bonus: He's *always* available!

your turn

❶
Name a time when you felt the Lord's comfort in the midst of a dilemma.

❷
Are you stressed about something today? If so, have you talked to God about it? (Now would be a good time!)

"Do not be anxious about anything, but in everything, by prayer and petition, with thanksgiving, present your requests to God. And the peace of God, which transcends all understanding, will guard your hearts and your minds in Christ Jesus."

PHILIPPIANS 4:6-7

EVERLASTING BEAUTY

Check It Out!
PROVERBS 31:30-31

My mother is beautiful. When I was a little girl I used to think she resembled a movie star—peaches-and-cream complexion, sparkling blue eyes, and a dazzling smile. On my grandma's piano, there's a photo of Mom that was taken during her college days. Every time I pass by it, I think about how it looks like it came straight out of the golden age of Hollywood. There's a hint of glamour to it that I've always found intriguing.

Years have passed since that photo was taken, and yet when I look at my mother today, I still see a beautiful woman. Of course she takes good care of herself and still has that Pepsodent smile, but the kind of beauty I'm talking about goes deeper than her outward appearance. I've come to realize that the true essence of my mother's elegance comes from the kind of person she is.

My mom has such a heart for God and for the people in her life. She's always been completely devoted to our family, and to me in particular. On a broader scale, for the past five years she has served as chairperson of the National Day of Prayer. These are a few aspects about my mom that make her the beautiful person that she is.

We've all seen gorgeous people who suddenly weren't very attractive when they opened their mouths. The opposite is true, too. I know a girl who doesn't have many physical attributes—her looks are plain and ordinary. But she wears makeup and clothes well, and she has a sense of confidence that permeates her being from head to toe. She also has a genuine love for the Lord that is evident in her personality. I've noticed that she never seems to have a problem attracting guys. It takes a lot more than looking like Tyra Banks or Cindy Crawford to be considered truly attractive.

Proverbs 31:30 says, "Charm is deceptive, and beauty is fleeting; but a woman who fears the Lord is to be praised."

Physical attractiveness is a temporary thing. It doesn't last. But does this mean that God expects you to ignore your appearance? Of course not! He understands how good it makes us feel to wear a new outfit or hear somebody say we look pretty. After all, quite often it's what's on the outside that makes someone want to get to know you better on the inside. Not enough can be said for first impressions.

There's nothing wrong with styling your hair, doing your nails, and keeping your clothes neat and clean. But don't lose sight of the greater priority. Spend time in prayer, read your Bible, and work at developing your relationship with the Lord. Then, just like my mother, you will have the kind of beauty that never fades.

your turn

①
Name someone that you consider to be beautiful. Why?

②
What is society's definition of beauty?

③
What do you think God's definition is?

④
What does beauty mean to you?

. . . AND I'M WORTH IT

Check It Out!
ROMANS 12:1-2

When I was in high school, it seemed like I was always battling "the big five." I'm talking about pounds, as you might have guessed. I know this doesn't sound like much weight, but have you ever picked up a five-pound bag of sugar or flour? It's an armload!

In order to combat this excess baggage, I invented my own daily 450-calorie diet (yes, I said 450!). It consisted of cottage cheese, a baked potato, fruit, chicken broth, and sherbet for dessert. It was both boring and nutritionally inadequate. Did I lose weight? Yes! Did I feel good? No! I walked around with no stamina, zero energy, and a craving for all foods forbidden. I could only endure this deprivation for about four days before gulping down a burger, fries, and a chocolate shake. I would then repeat the cycle until I lost the weight, and then I'd put it on again.

As ridiculous as that sounds, it's mild compared to what some girls have done to fight the battle of the bulge. I read that four supermodels were at Hard Rock Cafe, splitting one hamburger into four quarters. One actress ate so many carrots that her fingers turned orange, and model Christie Brinkley went on a yogurt-only diet for two weeks until she passed out! Some resort to even more drastic measures, such as starving themselves or binging and purging.

Why do women go to such extremes to be skinny? The obvious answer is that society pressures us to fit a certain image. Everything from commercials to catalogs sends us the message that bone-thin is in! Good examples of this are the Victoria's Secret models. Their slender, perfect bodies do not represent the average physique, and yet there they are—posed in a pair of underwear or even less. The advertising idea is that we can look just as sexy as those models if we buy the company's stuff. Maybe that's why two sisters that I know decided to forgo flipping through *Victoria's Secret* catalogs altogether. Wise girls!

This obsession with body image appears to have affected the late Princess Diana of the United Kingdom. In my dad's book *Bringing Up Boys,* he talked about Diana's dissatisfaction with her physical appearance. Diana, Princess of Wales, was arguably one of the most beautiful and glamorous women in the world. She was hounded by photographers right to the last moment, when a car accident took her life. During the latter years, Diana could raise more support for a particular cause or charity than any other celebrity. Given her enormous influence, along with her glamour and beauty, isn't it interesting that the princess disliked what she saw in the mirror? Diana struggled with a poor body image that led to an eating disorder known as bulimia. How could a woman of such charm fall victim to inferiority and depression?

Perhaps Diana's low self-concept wasn't as strange as it might have seemed. Our value system, prompted so vigorously by Hollywood and the entertainment industry, is arranged so that very few women feel good about their physical appearance. Even the Miss America or Miss Universe contestants will admit, if they're honest, that they are bothered by their physical flaws. If those who are blessed with great beauty and glamour often struggle with this problem, imagine how some teens must feel about the imperfect bodies with which they're born.

The beauty cult infects hundreds of millions of people with a sense of inadequacy. Indeed, even Princess Diana fell into its trap.

We're bombarded everywhere with images of gorgeous women with hot bodies. The implication is that it's not okay to be an average weight. It's unfortunate that so many women have bought into this propaganda. There are times when I still struggle with it myself.

What makes it worse is that many guys believe it, too. They want their girlfriends or wives to lose weight and live up to a celebrity standard of perfection. The truth is that females come in a *variety* of shapes and sizes. Not everyone is as small-boned as Britney Spears or Christina Aguilera; it's foolish to aspire to look like them.

It's interesting to note that fifty years ago, Marilyn Monroe was the ideal. With her average weight and curvy figure, she had the "look" that society admired. Marilyn would be considered chunky by today's standards. Modern girls are walking around much thinner than God ever intended them to be.

What a dilemma we face! All across the nation, millions of people are on diets right now. Even kids as young as eight, nine, and ten are trying to slim down. It's a pity when even elementary students concern themselves with weight-management. It takes the fun out of being a kid—and it is harmful physically.

I wonder how the Lord feels about all of this. The other day, I stumbled across a passage of Scripture that seems relevant to this subject: "Therefore, I urge you, brothers, in view of God's mercy, to offer your bodies as living sacrifices, holy and pleasing to God— this is your spiritual act of worship. Do not conform any longer to the pattern of this world, but be transformed by the renewing of your mind. Then you will be able to test and approve what God's will is—his good, pleasing and perfect will" (Romans 12:1-2).

Clearly, our bodies belong not to ourselves, but to God. He made us in His image, and our worth comes from Him. Therefore, our perception about ourselves should come from *Him*, not from a photo of waiflike Kate Moss.

One thing that I'm certain of is that God wants us to take care of our bodies. Too many fast-food meals, soft drinks, and candy bars can harm our health over time. On the other hand, we all know that eating protein, fresh fruits, and vegetables can help us feel good and stay healthy. Nutritious foods keep our energy up, our complexion glowing, our hair shiny, and our bodies functioning at their best. In addition to a well-balanced diet, it's also important to exercise. Working up a sweat while bicycling, swimming, or roller blading, for example, is not only beneficial for our health, but it also releases endorphins that make us feel happier and more energetic. In this fast-paced world, we need a good stressbuster!

A girl who takes care of herself has a greater chance of feeling good than someone who doesn't. But eating right and exercising isn't enough without spiritual health. We need to be communicating with God and spending time in His Word. The wonderful thing about talking to the Lord is that He is interested in every aspect of our lives. He isn't bored or distracted when we express our concerns about how we look. It says in Psalm 37:23 that the Lord delights in the way of man. Our body is His temple (1 Corinthians 6:19-20), and He wants us to maintain it properly.

As I'm writing this, I happen to be on yet another diet. Those five pounds are back! I'm happy to report, however, that I no longer suffer through insufficient "crash" meals. These days, when I want to take off a few, I make sure I cover the basic food groups and try to exercise. I also invite the Lord to help me to be disciplined. This is the best way to reach my fitness goals and feel good about myself. It goes along with what the apostle Paul urged us to do in 1 Corinthians 10:31: "So whether you eat or drink or whatever you do, do it all for the glory of God." That pretty much sums it up, don't you think?

your turn

1

Have you done anything unhealthy to try to lose weight? What did you do? How did it make you feel?

2

Do you think that society pressures us to resemble a certain image?

3

Is the Lord a part of your regular nutrition and exercise regimen? If not, consider giving Him full control!

A HUNGER FOR ACCEPTANCE

Check It Out!
GALATIANS 6:4

Shortly after her fourteenth birthday, Keri began to worry about her weight. Alarmed by how tight her jeans had become, Keri started a crash diet to shed the extra pounds. The results proved successful! Keri's self-confidence improved as family and friends remarked about how good she looked. Even the cute guy in her biology class was "checking her out." This was too good to be true!

Pleased with her new appearance, Keri continued her strict diet. She allowed herself no more than five hundred calories per day and worked herself to exhaustion on the stair-climbing machine. It wasn't long before she started to look undernourished and fatigued. Her concerned mother tried to convince her daughter that she was becoming too thin, but Keri didn't see herself from the same perspective. When she stood in front of her full-length mirror, all she saw were "hippo hips" and "thunder thighs."

As the days went by, Keri became more obsessed with counting calories. Whenever her mom placed a well-balanced meal in front of her, Keri would push food around the plate with her fork and hide morsels in her napkin. While sitting in biology class, she couldn't concentrate on her studies, and she no longer gave much thought to the cute guy she once admired. Instead she pondered what to eat after school—a carrot or a strawberry. She even worried about the calories in her toothpaste! When her menstrual cycle skipped a month, it didn't phase her; nothing could interfere with her get-thin mind-set. It wasn't until she collapsed during an afternoon aerobics class and was rushed to the hospital that Keri finally admitted she had a problem. The test results were conclusive: irregular heartbeat, low blood pressure, and loss of muscle tissue. Keri had to face the fact that she was battling an eating disorder called anorexia nervosa. It was time to get professional help.

During treatment, Keri learned that her struggle with anorexia really wasn't about wanting to be thin. There were deeper issues involved—issues that started years earlier.

As a young girl, Keri had witnessed the breakdown of her parents' marriage. The conflicts, the anger, and the insults were daily torment for a sensitive child. She had wanted to fix the problems and make everything better, but the situation was beyond her control. At the time, Keri assumed partial responsibility for the tension in her home. When she spilled a glass of milk or broke a dish, she felt guilty for causing her mom additional stress. Her parents finally divorced when Keri was nine years old. What followed was an estranged relationship with a busy father who was seldom available.

As Keri received godly counseling, she came to realize that behind her eating disorder was a need for acceptance and an overwhelming attempt to control her life. She discovered that these feelings were rooted in experiences from her past. Keri also learned of her heavenly Father's compassionate love for her—how He understood her struggle and wanted to bring her to a place of victory. She only needed to give Him control of her life.

Results didn't happen overnight. Learning to think and eat right was a process that took time, but now, one year later, Keri is on the road to recovery. She has gained fifteen pounds (now within a normal weight range for her height and bone structure), and she is eating healthy foods in regular-sized portions. Every day Keri reads God's Word and asks the Lord to help her in the battle with anorexia. As she daily surrenders her eating habits, her thoughts, and her life to Him, she is reminded of His power to save and change lives.

Do you know someone like Keri? Have you yourself dealt with some of the same issues? Perhaps your struggle is bulimia. This is another disorder in which the person "pigs out" and then forces herself to vomit. Bulimia is as destructive and harmful to the body as anorexia is. Girls who are bulimic may experience muscular weakness (including the heart), tooth decay and gum erosion, tears in the esophagus, fluid imbalance, vitamin deficiencies, and central nervous system disturbances. These symptoms are not to be taken lightly! Bulimia and anorexia are serious conditions that can prove fatal if left untreated.

Please don't say to yourself, "I can handle it on my own." The fact is that you cannot! If you're battling an eating disorder, it's essential that you receive medical, psychological, and nutritional treatment. You also need spiritual counsel! If you're unsure where to turn, talk to your parent(s), a close friend, or an authority figure whom you trust. Ask one of these people to help you find the right professional to meet your needs.

If you know a friend who is battling with an eating disorder, don't be afraid to confront that person. Express your concern in a loving way and offer to help. Do whatever you can to reach out to your friend—pray for her and make a copy of this chapter to share. Your efforts might be the beginning of a healing process for your friend.

The American culture sure is *obsessed* with physical perfection, isn't it? Everywhere we look—magazines, TV ads, movies—that message is being thrown at us (have you picked up a fashion catalog lately?). Somewhere along the way we have bought into the lie that being thin and beautiful is a guarantee of happiness. Wrong! Genuine happiness comes from within, and only Jesus can provide it—not a pair of stretch denim jeans!

Jesus said He came that we "may have life, and have it to the full" (John 10:10). It is His desire that we come to a place of peace and acceptance with our bodies as He made them. Naturally, this doesn't mean that we shouldn't take care of ourselves, but dieting and exercise should stay within a healthy boundary.

Do you have a weakness in this area? If you do, then check out what the apostle Paul had to say in 2 Corinthians 12:9-10: "Therefore I will boast all the more gladly about my weaknesses, so that Christ's power may rest on me. That is why, for Christ's sake, I delight in weaknesses, in insults, in hardships, in persecutions, in difficulties. For when I am weak, then I am strong." No matter what your struggles are, admit them to the Lord and ask Him to teach you the right way to live. He will give you His strength to make good decisions each day.

your turn

1

Have you felt pressure from our society to fit a "mold" or a specific body image?

2

What is the need behind a person's struggle wth anorexia or bulimia?

3

Do you believe that God can help someone overcome an eating disorder, no matter how intense it is?

WHEN I GROW UP, I WANT TO BE . . .

Check It Out!
PROVERBS 3:5-6

When you were a little girl, you probably thought about what you wanted to be when you grew up—a missionary, a veterinarian, a mommy. Those vague ambitions might have changed as you grew older, but your dreams for the future are still alive in your heart.

Did you know that God has an interest in your future, as well? Consider His promise to the Israelites in Jeremiah 29:11-14: "'For I know the plans I have for you,' declares the Lord, 'plans to prosper you and not to harm you, plans to give you hope and a future. Then you will call upon me and come and pray to me, and I will listen to you. You will seek me and find me when you seek me with all your heart. I will be found by you,' declares the Lord."

Isn't that an encouraging and comforting passage? The God of the universe, who is all-powerful and all-knowing, loves and cares for each of His children and has a wonderful plan for our lives! If we're walking in obedience and seeking His will, all we have to do is trust Him to reveal His plan for us.

This seems easy to do, but unfortunately, it can also be a struggle at times. We want to be the master of our own destiny. We don't want to let God lead, because His plans are often out of step with our own. I speak from experience at this point, because I've had to overcome my desire to have it *my* way!

When I was in high school, I remember telling family and friends that I wanted to get married at a certain age, have kids a few years later, and enjoy a career that generated a six-figure income. As it turned out, I've remained single while my friends from college went on to exchange vows and have babies. As far as that six-figure income . . . well . . . let's just say that I'm more realistic now.

Obviously, my life has taken some unanticipated turns in the road. I still believe the Lord wants to give me the desires of my heart (Psalm 37:4), but I've had to conform them to His purposes. Tough assignment!

I heard a pastor say that God's main thrust for our lives is not our happiness and satisfaction. It is His desire that we live according to His perfect will, which is *always* in our best interest. When we're in sync with God's plan, we can rest assured that it's the ideal situation—even if it doesn't make sense or meet our approval.

My grandfather struggled as a teenager with the will of God. He had known from an early age that he wanted to be an artist—nothing was going to stand in his way. During his senior year of high school, he began thinking about where he wanted to attend college. One day as he was walking down the street, he had a strong sense that God was asking him to lay aside his dream and become a minister. He was alarmed by this message! "No, no, Lord," he pleaded. "You know that I have my plans all made, and art is my consuming interest!" Then he tried to ignore what he felt God calling him to do, but the impression would not go away.

Finally, after wrestling with "the call" for months, the boy who was to become my grandfather made the decision to pursue his own interests. He said to God, "It's too great a price, and I won't pay it!" He soon enrolled in a prestigious art school and became best student in his class. On graduation day, his paintings were displayed on the platform with a "Number One" banner draped across them. But as he was walking down the aisle to receive his degree, he was reminded of this Scripture: "Unless the Lord builds the house, its builders labor in vain" (Psalm 127:1).

To make a long story short, my grandfather hit hard times in the 1930s during the Great Depression. This was a tough period in our history when many people were out of work. After pumping gas for "peanuts," my grandpa yielded his life to the Lord. He accepted the call to preach and began preparing for the ministry.

Does it seem cruel of God to deprive this young man of what he truly wanted? Why would the Lord give him unique talent and then prevent him from using it? Well, as is always the case in the Lord's dealings with us, God had my grandfather's best interests at heart. He took nothing away from him!

Once my grandpa submitted to what the Lord wanted, his art was given back to him. He then used his talent in ministerial work all his life, and when he died, he was chairman of the art department at a Christian college. He created beautiful paintings and sculptures, including one that holds a prominent place in my home. More importantly, thousands of people came to know Jesus Christ through the preaching ministry of my grandfather. They will be in heaven because of the calling that was on his life.

So you see, that terrible struggle during his teen years was not a cruel manipulation. It was a test to see if my grandfather would allow God to be in control of his life. There was nothing sinful or immoral in his love of art, but it outranked his relationship with the Lord. He needed to have a change of heart.

Jesus Christ will require that of you, too. He will be Lord of all or not Lord at all. It's natural to have goals and interests, but keep an open mind to the leading of the Holy Spirit. Don't get so determined to have your own way (like my grandfather) that you ignore the small voice inside!

The most important thing you can do is pray about your decisions. The Scriptures tell us that He will hear your prayers and help you see the wonderful plan described in Jeremiah 29:11. Read it again and consider these additional verses:

"Trust in the Lord with all your heart, and do not lean on your own understanding. In all your ways acknowledge Him, and He will make your paths straight" (Proverbs 3:5-6, NASB).

"Whether you turn to the right or the left, your ears will hear a voice behind you, saying, 'This is the way; walk in it'" (Isaiah 30:21).

"But seek first His kingdom and His righteousness; and all these things shall be added to you" (Matthew 6:33, NASB).

I don't know about you, but these Scriptures make me want to breathe a sigh of relief. What a comfort to know that our lives are in God's hands—we can trust His plan with assurance!

your turn

①

What would you like to do with your life? Have you prayed for direction?

②

How will you respond if God's plan is out of sync with your own?

③

Have you given the Lord total control of your destiny? If not, pray now that His will would be done in your life.

Let's talk about ETERNITY!

Stand or Fall

STAND OR FALL

Check It Out!
JOHN 5:24

We come now to the final entry in this book about relationships and how you can make them healthy and more meaningful. I hope you have found these forty discussions helpful as we talked about God, your parents, brothers and sisters, your friends, you, and of course, about guys. The ideas I have shared with you have come not only from my own personal experiences but also from the wisdom of the Scriptures. I hope you have seen that the Bible is amazingly applicable to our personal lives, providing direction that is as current and usable now as when it was written long ago. You can trust the Bible to guide your steps throughout life.

I would like to conclude our time together by asking a few questions about *the* most important relationship that you or I will ever have:

- Do you know with certainty what you believe about God and how He fits into your life?
- Do you have a clear idea of who God is and what He expects you to do?
- Is Jesus Christ real and alive in your heart, or do you believe He is just a prophet who lived two thousand years ago and said some nice things about love and peace?
- If you died today, would you go to heaven? If so, why?

Have you taken time to consider these questions about your faith and how your basic beliefs influence the way you live?

If you are like millions of other teens, you are probably fuzzy about some of the eternal issues I have raised. You may have gone to church since you were a baby but still do not comprehend what it all means. Or maybe you haven't spent much time in a church, but you'd like to get closer to God. Either way, it might be helpful for us to think together about your relationship with God—and how that understanding translates into meaning for every other aspect of your life.

The reason this discussion is so important is that now, more than ever, we are surrounded by off-the-wall philosophies and theologies that are contradictory to everything taught in Scripture. The "beautiful people" in the entertainment industry, in the media, and in the culture at large are promoting New Age stuff that would have been considered crazy by previous generations. For example, I visited a bookstore a few days ago and found more than forty titles in the New Age section that explored witchcraft. There were also resources on astrology, numerology, psychic discoveries, tarot-card reading, reincarnation, and futuristic healing, among other things. Four books were written specifically for "teenage witches"! Each one contained a bevy of magic spells for everything from parental conflicts to menstrual cramps. I also found some kits on the shelves—little boxes of trinkets that girls could use to cast spells.

What disturbs me is that these godless ideas have become faddish for teens. Some students walk around with crystals dangling from their necks, believing that certain stones give off specific types of energies. Others think there is spiritual power in a potion of jasmine, ribbon, and dried sage. Yet there is absolutely no evidence, scientific or otherwise, that supports these notions. Nevertheless, people who believe in them are trying to fill an emptiness in their soul that longs for meaning and purpose. In the absence of a personal relationship with God, it's tempting to seek mystical answers in the occult. But it's like leaning on the wind.

Let me tell you that *the real power in life comes from Jesus Christ!*

Not surprisingly, none of the literature I explored even mentioned His name. Most of the stuff promised "power" and "peace," but without Christ, these materials can only produce confusion and emptiness. They also can't change how people feel about themselves or how they treat others.

You may remember that we covered the subject of postmodernism a while ago. This is another common way of thinking that is just as dangerous as New Age philosophy. It is based on the belief that there is no God and that human beings are simply accidents of nature in a chaotic universe. Its adherents say there is nothing right or wrong, moral or immoral, good or bad. Each person makes up his or her own rules and standards. Another name for this is "moral relativism," and it is what you will most likely be taught if you go to a secular university after high school. King Solomon wrote about this distorted way of thinking in Proverbs 14:12. He said, "There is a way that seems right to a man, but in the end it leads to death."

What about you? Do you know what you believe, and is that understanding backed by Scripture? Will you be able to explain or defend your beliefs if a teacher or professor challenges you in class? This is extremely important, for as the Lord said in Isaiah 7:9, "If you do not stand firm in your faith, you will not stand at all."

I'm reminded of the story that Jesus told about a foolish man who built his house upon the sand (Matthew 7:24-27). Because the foundation was weak, the structure collapsed when the storm raged. On the other hand, there was also a man who built upon a rock. His house was on solid ground, so it was able to withstand the harsh beating from the storm. Jesus told this parable to encourage you to put His words into practice. By doing so, you are strengthening your faith. As Paul wrote in 2 Corinthians 1:24: "It is by faith you stand firm."

I have a friend whose house was sitting on wet sand. He grew up in the church and called himself a Christian, but somewhere in his twenties he wandered from the truth. He dated one girl who practiced the New Age philosophy and another who was Jewish. He himself explored Buddhism, often reading books on the subject and spending time in ashrams (places of worship for people of different faiths). During one conversation I had with him, he tried to convince me that, in a religious sense, "all roads lead to Rome." What he was saying, in essence, is that every religion is acceptable to God. I reminded him of Jesus' words in John 14:6: "I am the way and the truth and the life. No one comes to the Father except through me." (Hardly an inclusive statement!) Furthermore, I told my friend that Christianity really isn't about religion as much as it is about *relationship*. I assured him that if he would give it all up for Jesus and get to know Him personally, he would discover the meaning of truth.

May I suggest that this is the time, if you haven't done so before, to establish your belief system on the solid, unshakable Rock of Jesus Christ? Let's do that by considering what are called the "fundamentals of the faith," which will lead you into a wonderful relationship with the Lord:

❶ Every person who has ever lived—including me and you—was born a sinner. Sin is anything we do, think, or say that displeases God or breaks His laws. Because of our impurity, there is nothing we can do to save ourselves or to earn our way into heaven, "for all have sinned and fall short of the glory of God" (Romans 3:23).

❷ God is holy and cannot tolerate wickedness, but He is also a loving Father who does not want to punish His children eternally. Therefore, He sent His Son, Jesus, to die in our place and provide a remedy for our sin. "For God so loved the world that he gave his one and only Son, that whoever believes in him shall not perish but have eternal life" (John 3:16).

❸ Jesus Christ, by His death on the cross, offers forgiveness to anyone who "repents" and believes on His name. Repentance is having sorrow for sin and a determination to turn from it. Jesus said, "Unless you repent, you too will all perish" (Luke 13:3). The apostle Peter said it like this: "Repent and be baptized, every one of you, in the name of Jesus Christ for the forgiveness of your sins. And you will receive the gift of the Holy Spirit" (Acts 2:38).

❹ After we enter into a relationship with Jesus Christ, He reigns on the throne of our lives as we yield our heart, mind, and soul to Him. He must be Lord of all, or He will not be Lord at all.

❺ Jesus has commanded all of his followers to "go into all the world and preach the good news to all creation" (Mark 16:15). This is called the "Great Commission." To do this we must study the Bible so that we know what it says and then watch for opportunities to tell others about what the Lord has done in our life. "Always be prepared to give an answer to everyone who asks you to give the reason for the hope that you have" (1 Peter 3:15).

Because Jesus rose from the dead, we too will do the same eventually. Eternal life in heaven will be ours, not because we have lived a perfect life, but because our debt of sin has been paid. We will live forever with God and with our friends and family who also are believers in Christ. Jesus said this: "I tell you the truth, whoever hears my word and believes him who sent me has eternal life and will not be condemned; he has crossed over from death to life" (John 5:24).

If you want to accept these marvelous gifts of forgiveness and eternal life, you can say a prayer like this: "Lord, I am so sorry for the wickedness in my life and the times that I have disappointed you. I believe that You died for my sins and rose from the dead to give me eternal life. Thank You for taking the punishment that I deserve. Please forgive me and come to live in my heart right now. I will do my best to serve You faithfully and to tell others about what You have done for me. I now belong to You forever. Amen."

If you prayed that prayer sincerely, guess what? You are now a child of God!

May I urge you now to get into a good Bible study with a teacher who knows the Word and can help you apply it to your life? The apostle Paul wrote, "Do your best to present yourself to

God as one approved, a workman who does not need to be ashamed and who correctly handles the word of truth" (2 Timothy 2:15). In other words, study the Bible!

With that, we will end. I would love to hear from you if you would like to write. You can reach me at Focus on the Family, Colorado Springs, CO, 80920.

ABOUT THE AUTHOR

 Danae Dobson was born in Southern California and wrote her first children's manuscript, *Woof! A Bedtime Story About a Dog,* when she was only twelve years of age.

She received her bachelor's degree in communication from Azusa Pacific University. She has authored twenty children's books to date, including the popular Woof series that followed the success of her original story. Other works include *Parables for Kids* (co-authored with Dr. James Dobson), the Forest Friends series, and the Sunny Street Kids' Club series.

Danae has appeared on the *700 Club* and other television shows and has been a guest on more than fifty radio broadcasts, including *Minirth Meier* and *Focus on the Family.* She has also been a featured speaker for such organizations as the Christian Booksellers Association, Hawaiian Island Ministries, and M.O.P.S.

Danae is the daughter of Dr. James and Shirley Dobson, and has a younger brother, Ryan. She still lives in Southern California and is active in her speaking ministry, conducting workshops, addressing women's groups, and visiting Christian schools.